W9-CAS-909

Making Handbags & Purses

50 Patterns & Designs from Casual to Corporate

Carol Parks

Lark Books
Asheville, North Carolina

Art and production: Kathleen Holmes
Photography: Evan Bracken, Light Reflections
Illustrations: Bernadette Wolf
Editorial assistance: Catharine Sutherland and Valerie Anderson
Editorial assistance and modeling: Evans Carter

Library of Congress Cataloging-in-Publication Data

Parks, Carol
    Making handbags & purses : 50 patterns & designs from casual to
corporate / Carol Parks. -- 1st ed.
      p.   cm.
    Includes index.
    ISBN 1-57990-012-7
    1. Handbags. 2. Sewing. 3. Fancy work. I. Title
TT667.P37 1997
646.4'8--dc21   97-31145
                        CIP

10 9 8 7 6 5 4 3 2

Published by Lark Books
50 College Street
Asheville, North Carolina 28801, USA

©1998 Lark Books

Distributed by Random House, Inc., in the United States, Canada,
    the United Kingdom, Europe, and Asia

Distributed in Australia by Capricorn Link (Australia) Pty Ltd.,
    P.O. Box 6651, Baulkham Hills Business Centre, NSW 2153, Australia

Distributed in New Zealand by Tandem Press Ltd., 2 Rugby Rd.,
    Birkenhead, Auckland, New Zealand

The written instructions, photographs, designs, patterns, and projects in
this volume are intended for the personal use of the reader and may be
reproduced for that purpose only. Any other use, especially commercial use,
is forbidden under law without written permission of the copyright holder.

Every effort has been made to ensure that all the information in this book
is accurate. However, due to differing conditions, tools, and individual
skills, the publisher cannot be responsible for any injuries, losses, or other
damages that may result from the use of the information in this book.

Printed in Hong Kong by Oceanic Graphic Printing, Ltd.

All rights reserved

ISBN 1-57990-012-7

CONTENTS

INTRODUCTION

There are any number of good reasons to make a handbag, as if a sewer ever needs a reason to make a beautiful thing. The bag you make can be better in many ways than one you could buy. You can choose luxurious materials and unique closures and findings. You can add all kinds of embellishment if you wish. You can make the bag a size and shape that suit you exactly. You can include pockets that precisely accommodate the things you will put into them. Whether you plan to duplicate a favorite bag that has seen better days, or put to use a special piece of fabric or needlework, or just spend an entertaining evening with your sewing machine, the bag you make can be just perfect!

DESIGNING A BAG

When you plan to make a bag, think about the way it will be used. Will it be an everyday bag meant to carry work to and from the office? A purse to use with your favorite out-to-dinner outfit? A custom-designed bag to take on a long vacation? Think about what will go into the bag—the weight as well as the volume. Plan from the inside out, choosing materials that are compatible with the bag's purpose. For a large bag that you plan to use regularly for a number of years, you will want durable fabric not just for the outer shell, but for the lining too. The strap or handles should be equally durable, and the zipper or closure should be strong enough to last the life of the bag itself.

A bag to be used infrequently, or a small one that need not carry much weight, can be made of almost anything. It is still a good idea to work outward from the interior, planning lining pockets to accommodate the items that you always carry with you.

As often as not, we design our sewing projects around an idea, a piece of fabric, or a unique closure rather than a real need for the finished item. Handbags, with their small fabric requirements, are a wonderful form of expression.

BEAUTIFUL GLASS BEADS PROVIDED THE DESIGN INSPIRATION FOR THIS SMALL BAG.

FABRICS FOR HANDBAGS

The function of the bag is the main consideration when it comes to choosing a fabric. For a working bag that will carry a heavy load and that must survive a good bit of wear and tear, you will want a sturdy, durable fabric. Heavyweight cotton or linen and firmly woven synthetics are good choices. Upholstery fabrics can work very well too. Remnants too small for upholstery projects often can be found at bargain prices. Avoid pieces with a stiff or rubbery backing; they are difficult for a home sewing machine to manage.

For bags that won't take such abuse, almost any fabric can work. Throughout the following chapters are examples of bags made of every conceivable fabric, including some very unlikely materials used in very clever ways.

And don't rule out leather. Its strength and good looks have made it the preferred material for purses and bags for a long time. It is not difficult to sew—there are some good tips on page 19 that will ease your mind if you have never worked with it. Mail order sources for garment-weight leathers advertise in sewing magazines and offer some beautiful choices, including machine-washable skins.

The fabric can provide a reason to make a bag in the first place. An heirloom tapestry too worn to display, a great flea market find, or even material from an out-of-style garment can be converted into a gorgeous and practical purse.

LININGS AND UNDERLININGS

Many of us have, stored away on a closet shelf, one magnificent bag that cost us a week's pay and saw many years of service. Its outer appearance is still handsome, but the inside! The lining is in shreds, ready to swallow up every coin and earring tossed its way.

Lining fabric should, and can, last as long as the outer fabric of the bag. The fabrics should be compatible in weight and cleaning or laundering requirements. The lining will be seen most often by you, so choose a fabric that gives you pleasure.

If you have ever tried in vain to find a pen or lipstick at the bottom of your handbag in a discretely lighted restaurant, you may wonder why manufacturers inevitably choose black lining

A LINING CAN MATCH THE BAG FABRIC, OR IT CAN PROVIDE A WONDERFUL CONTRAST.

fabric. A brightly colored lining has advantages beyond just the aesthetic ones.

The outer bag fabric and lining together should be thick enough that the bag's contents won't create unsightly protuberances visible from the outside. Underlining or backing applied to the outer shell also adds stability to the fabric. Garment-weight batting is the choice of many of the designers. It is soft and lightweight, and it adds just a little thickness. It is available in both fusible and sew-in forms.

Interlining—batting or other fabric used as backing for the lining rather than the outer shell—is sometimes a better choice. The outer fabric may need no additional weight or stability, but the lining might be nicer with the added body provided by another layer of fabric. Interlining can be cut by the lining pattern, then sewn as one with the lining.

POCKETS

VERTICAL LINES OF STITCHING DIVIDE A SINGLE PATCH POCKET INTO SECTIONS TO KEEP THE BAG'S CONTENTS ORDERLY.

The option of adding custom-designed pockets is one of the best reasons of all for making a handbag. Whatever items you need to carry can be stored safely exactly where you can find them. The bags on the following pages feature a good variety of pocket styles for a bag's exterior. It is on the lining, though, that you can provide for organizing your gear. Whether you need a place to keep sunglasses handy or a secure pocket for a passport, you can design a perfect pocket or several for the lining of almost any purse.

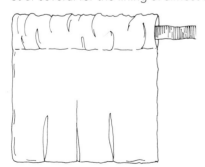

ADD AN INCH OR TWO TO THE INTENDED FINISHED WIDTH OF A PATCH POCKET AND FOLD THE EXCESS INTO PLEATS AT THE BOTTOM FOR EASE. USE THE UPPER HEM AS A CASING FOR ELASTIC.

When you plan pockets for a lining, allow generous ease so that the pocket, when filled, will expand toward the bag's interior. If the contents are forced toward the exterior, the bag will look lumpy.

Patch pockets are the quickest to make. Cut a rectangle of fabric, adding enough to the width to make a pleat for ease, and adding seam and hem allowances. A patch pocket can be almost the full width of the lining piece and subdivided with vertical lines of stitching, or it can be sized to hold just a pencil or credit cards. It might call for a button at the top, or it could be secured with a fabric-covered snap or hook and loop tape.

A zippered pocket provides for secure storage, and takes little extra time to make. A zipper with nylon coils can easily be shortened as you require—just cut off the excess length at the upper end after you stitch the zipper in place.

To add a zipper toward the top of a patch pocket, cut the pocket as two pieces of equal width. Cut the upper piece for a finished length of approximately 3/4 inch (2 cm), adding seam allowances on all sides. Make the lower section the length you want the pocket to be, with seam allowances on all sides.

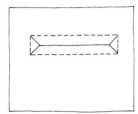

STITCH A WINDOW TO INSTALL A ZIPPER, THEN CUT AS INDICATED AND PRESS UNDER THE EDGES.

Sew a horizontal edge of each fabric piece to the zipper, right sides together, aligning the fabric seamline with the stitching line on the zipper tape. Press the seam allowance toward the zipper tape, then topstitch.

A zipper can easily be installed in a single piece of fabric too. Mark a rectangle on the fabric, slightly longer and wider than the zipper teeth. Stitch around the marked line with a fairly short stitch. Cut as shown. Press under the raw edges. Center the zipper behind the opening and stitch close to the folded edges.

This method can be used to install a zipper in the pocket, or in the lining itself. In the latter case, sew the pocket to the wrong side of the lining, stitching around all edges.

STRAPS AND HANDLES

A stitched tube of self fabric, turned right side out and topstitched along the long edges, makes a perfectly effective strap for a shoulder bag. For a heavy bag especially, it is a good idea to add a strip of interfacing to help prevent stretching.

A FINE TWISTED CORD DRAWSTRING, MADE WITH THE SAME SILK THREAD USED FOR THE SMOCKING, SUITS THE DIMENSIONS OF THIS ELEGANT EVENING BAG.

Sew the strap securely to the bag. If the ends are sewn into a seam, add several rows of stitching in the seam allowance for security. When the strap ends are sewn to the inside or outside of the bag, topstitch at least an inch of each end in place, then stitch an X (or some pattern) within the topstitched area.

For some interesting alternatives to a basic fabric strap, look what these designers have chosen. Braided yarn, purchased chains of every description, cording and ribbons—all are good options. As long as the strap suits the bag design and weight, is comfortable to wear, and pleases you, anything goes!

Twisted cord made of yarn or threads used on the body of the bag creates a beautiful custom strap. To make twisted cord, cut lengths of yarn approximately three times the desired length of the finished cord. The finished cord will be approximately three times the diameter of the strands you start with.

Tie one end of the bunch of strands to a doorknob, or get a friend to hold it. Keeping the yarn taut, twist the strands until they are evenly twisted along the length. Then, still holding the cord taut, fold it double and allow it to twist upon itself. Knot the ends together.

FINDINGS AND CLOSURES

THE BAG FABRIC, IN THIS CASE LEATHER, CAN BE USED IN PLACE OF TRADITIONAL METAL FINDINGS TO ATTACH THE STRAP TO THE BAG.

A number of the bags shown in this book were planned around their unique closures. For a small bag particularly, the closure can be the focal point of the design. A wonderful antique button or an interesting bit of knotwork might inspire a purse that will be a longtime favorite.

Suppliers of traditional handbag findings often advertise in sewing magazines and offer a good selection of hardware by mail. But there are plenty of alternatives to the traditional closures and fasteners. Look in hardware

PEWTER BEADS, KNOTTED ONTO THE THREAD USED TO PLEAT THE BAG OPENING ADD A SPECIAL DESIGN ELEMENT.

stores, salvage shops, flea markets, and the basement workshop for hooks and nuts and bolts that will fit nicely into—or inspire—a handbag design.

THE FINISHING TOUCH

Just like a custom garment, a handmade bag is made truly special by the addition of one or two "unnecessary" details. Stitch your own label to a lining pocket, or embroider the recipient's monogram if the bag will be a gift. Use a silk-covered snap instead of a hook and loop tape closure.

FINISHING TOUCHES MAKE A BAG UNIQUE. HERE, THE LINING WAS ATTACHED WITH HAND EMBROIDERY, AND THE BUTTON LOOP WAS MADE WITH YARNS USED TO WEAVE THE BAG.

Try painting or stenciling the lining fabric. String a few freshwater pearls to make a zipper pull.

Tassels are fun to add, and many of our designers have used them as accents for their bags. A tassel can be made quickly with medium-weight yarn. It can be left fairly plain, or elaborately embellished with beads, decorative threads, and embroidery stitches as the designers have done.

To make a simple tassel, cut a piece of cardboard the width of the intended finished length of the tassel. Wrap yarn or thread around the cardboard to the desired thickness. Tie the strands together at one edge of the cardboard, then cut through them at the other edge. Smooth the strands down at the point where they are tied, and wrap the bundle tightly to form the neck and head of the tassel.

If the tassel will be at the end of a cord, as for a strap or zipper pull, tie an overhand knot at the end of the cord and slip it through the thread used to tie the strands. The knot will fill out the head of the tassel.

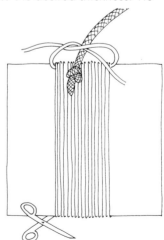

TO ATTACH THE TASSEL TO A CORD, SLIP THE KNOTTED CORD THROUGH THE THREAD USED TO TIE THE YARN STRANDS.

CHAPTER 1

ENVELOPE BAGS IN MANY STYLES

A basic envelope may be the simplest kind of purse to construct, but as you can see by the photos on the following pages, the designs can range from simple to quite sophisticated. The addition of a flap or unusual placement of a zipper can completely change the look of the bag. One made of a bright floral print fabric has a very different character than the same style made of neutral linen. And there is endless potential for embellishment, of course!

Linen Envelope

The design is tailored and quite sophisticated, with just the right amount of embellishment. Small ivory beads and couched nubby silk yarn complement the natural linen fabric beautifully. The zipper, instead of being placed predictably along the top, is at the upper back of the bag where it becomes an element of the overall design.

With a soft neutral color like this, a bright lining is fun. A shoulder strap could be added easily, made of the bag fabric or braided strands of the yarn, sewn into the side seams.

The bag is 10 by 8 inches (25.5 by 20 cm).

MATERIALS

Fabric for outer bag: medium-weight linen or other fabric, 11 by 20 inches (28 by 51 cm) and small scraps

Lining: a rectangle the size of the outer bag piece

Zipper: 9 inches (23 cm)

Yarn for couching

Assorted beads

CONSTRUCTION

Use 1/2 inch (1.5 cm) seam allowance except as otherwise noted.

1. Cut two 2-1/2-inch (6.5-cm) squares of the outer bag fabric scraps. Fold each diagonally, right sides together, matching edges. Stitch with a very narrow seam allowance. Trim the corner. Cut along the fold and turn right side out; press.

2. Press under the seam allowances on the short ends of the outer bag piece. The zipper will be installed in this seam. Determine placement for the zipper seam and mark the folds at the bag top and bottom. Allow approximately 1 inch (2.5 cm) on each side of the lower fold; this area will be at the bottom of the bag.

3. Design the decorative elements. To couch yarn, as in this design, use a fairly wide zigzag stitch at a medium-long length setting. Use a cording foot to guide the yarn, or an

Designer: **Lori Kerr**

one end of the zipper teeth, the raw edge in the seam allowance. Edgestitch in place.

6. Open the zipper a little. With right sides together, stitch the side seams.

7. At the bottom, fold each corner to a point, centering the seam. Stitch across, exactly perpendicular to the seamline and approximately 1-1/4 inches (3.5 cm) in from the end of the seam as shown.

8. For the lining, press under the end seam allowances as for the outer bag. Fold the piece with right sides together, orienting the pressed edges to correspond with the zipper in the bag.

9. Pin, then stitch the sides seams, leaving approximately 1/4 inch (.7 cm) space between the folded ends. Stitch across the points at the bottom of the side seams as for the bag.

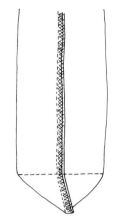

TO SQUARE THE LOWER CORNERS, FOLD A POINT AND STITCH PERPENDICULAR TO THE SEAMLINE.

10. Place the lining in the bag and whipstitch the lining edges along the zipper tape.

11. For an intriguing zipper pull, attach beads to the zipper tab with a strand of yarn.

embroidery foot. Guide the yarn so the needle doesn't catch it in the stitches. This designer used black thread in the bobbin and tightened the upper thread tension so the bobbin stitches would show slightly. The beads also were sewn with black thread for contrast.

If the fabric is too light in weight to support the decorative stitching, try using a lightweight interfacing, or spray with a little starch before sewing.

4. When the decorative stitching is finished, install the zipper. With the zipper right side up, position one of the folded edges of the bag piece right side up over the edge of the zipper tape. Allow approximately 3/16 inch (.5 cm) between the fold and the center of the zipper teeth for an exposed zipper as shown. Stitch close to the fold. Stitch the other side in the same way.

5. Position each fabric triangle with the point at the

BAG DU JOUR

This small bag is so uncomplicated to make that you can stitch a different interpretation for each day of the week. And there are so many possible color and fabric combinations that you'll never run short of ideas.

This model is made of a scrap of rough silk fabric. Cotton, in a tapestry print, was used for the binding and appliqué and for the covered button and its loop. The lining is lightweight cotton with a checked pattern that coordinates with the tapestry print. The fabric layers are held together with free-motion stitching, described on page 14. Matching

thread was used for much of the stitching so that only the altered fabric texture is noticed. Details stitched in the tapestry print colors accent the appliqué, and a few drops of glitter glue provide a bit of sparkle.

The size is variable; the design would work just as well for a much larger bag (widen the strap to support the weight of a bigger one). The model shown is 6 inches (15 cm) wide and 5 inches (12.5 cm) high. The strap is 32 inches (81.5 cm) long, and can easily be made the length you like.

Designer: KAREN SWING

MATERIALS

Fabric for the outer bag, a rectangle approximately 7-1/2 by 14 inches (19 by 35 cm)

Lining fabric, the size of the outer bag

Garment-weight batting or cotton flannel, the size of the outer bag

Complementary fabric for binding, strap, and appliqué, approximately 1/4 yard (.25 m)

Button to cover

Optional: glitter glue

CONSTRUCTION

The fabric pieces are cut slightly larger than needed for the finished dimensions and will be trimmed to size after the layers are stitched. Allow for this when planning a design.

Stitching and decorating the layers

1. Layer the fabric rectangles, the outer fabric and lining right side out and the batting between. Pin baste together.

2. To stabilize the fabric for stitching, spray-starch one side of the piece, allow it to dry, then starch the other side. Starch the appliqué fabric lightly.

3. Cut a motif from the contrast fabric for the appliqué and glue-baste it toward one end (the flap) of the outer fabric.

4. Using the free-motion stitching technique described on page 14, stitch the appliqué in place and stitch over the entire piece to hold the layers together. Add detail stitching with other thread colors if you wish.

5. When the stitching is complete, trim the rectangle to 6-1/2 by 13 inches (16.5 by 33 cm).

Assembly

1. With right sides together, fold the lower edge of the bag upward by 4-1/2 inches (11.5 cm). Stitch the sides, using 1/4 inch (.7 cm) seam allowance. Overcast the seam allowances neatly. Turn.

2. Trim the sides of the flap so they are slightly narrower than the finished front of the bag as shown. Round the corners slightly at the upper edges of the opening.

TRIM THE FLAP SO IT IS SLIGHTLY NARROWER THAN THE BAG FRONT.

3. Finish the raw edges with an overcast or zigzag stitch, or serge them.

Edge binding and finishing

1. Cut strips 1-1/2 inches (4 cm) wide for the binding and strap. Strips for the edge binding can be cut on the bias, if you wish, for smoother application. The strap should be cut on the lengthwise grain to prevent it stretching too much. You will need a total length of approximately 61 inches (155 cm).

2. Cut a strip for the button loop. A 4-inch (10-cm) strip will accommodate a button 1-1/4 inches (3.2 cm) in diameter. Press the strip in half lengthwise, then press the raw edges in to the center. Stitch close to both edges. Fold the strip to form a point, as shown. Position at the center of the flap edge on the right side.

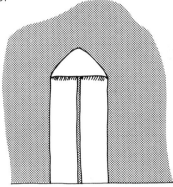

FOR A NEAT BUTTON LOOP, SEW THE ENDS OF A STITCHED FABRIC TUBE INTO THE EDGE BINDING SEAM.

3. For the strap, sew the long edges of the strip, right sides together, using 1/4 inch (.7 cm) seam allowance. Turn and press. Alternatively, press folds and stitch as for the button loop. Align the strap ends with the front edge of the bag near the side seamlines.

4. Beginning on the front, stitch the binding strip to the bag, right sides together and edges aligned, using 3/8 inch (1 cm) seam allowance. At the flap/front corners, ease the fabric and clip into the seam allowances as necessary. Miter the flap corners. Fold under the overlapping end. Press binding toward the seam allowances.

5. Fold under the raw edge of the strip so the fold just covers the previous stitching line and stitch by hand.

6. Cover the button and sew it on the bag front.

Designer: LIZ SPEAR

HANDWOVEN BAG

An especially beautiful fabric deserves to be seen. This designer, a professional weaver, chose a simple style for her purse and repeated the rich color of the fabric in the cord and button, and for the lining. The button is an especially nice detail. A small bead was sewn above it, with a flatter bead below to accommodate the thickness of the button loop.

We may not all have access to handwoven fabric, but this bag design offers a wonderful opportunity to put to practical use those treasured fabric pieces that are too small for other projects. Choose a rather heavy, fairly soft fabric such as silk or cotton coating, or even upholstery fabric as long as it is not too stiff. For the cord, blend cotton, rayon, or silk weaving or knitting yarns that coordinate with the fabric colors.

The finished bag is 10-1/2 inches (26.5 cm) wide and 7-1/4 inches (18.5 cm) high.

MATERIALS

Fabric, for outer bag: a rectangle 11-1/2 by 17 inches (29 by 43 cm)

Garment-weight batting: a rectangle 11 by 16 inches (28 by 40.5 cm)

Lining fabric: 3/8 yard (.35 m)

Assorted yarn for the cord and button loop

Button

INSTRUCTIONS

Seam allowances are 1/2 inch (1.5 cm) unless otherwise noted.

1. For the strap, make a length of twisted cord approximately 3/8 inch (1 cm) in diameter and 46 inches (117 cm) long. For the button loop, make a 6-inch (15-cm) cord smaller in diameter. (Twisted cord instructions are on page 6.)

2. For the lining, cut a rectangle the size of the batting.

3. Make pockets from the lining fabric and stitch them in place. Keep in mind that the short ends of the lining piece will be at the upper edges of the bag.

4. Baste the batting to the wrong side of the lining, just outside the seamlines. Trim the batting close to the stitching.

5. Fold the piece crosswise, right sides together, and stitch the sides. At each lower corner, fold a triangle, making a point at the lower end of the seam. Stitch across the point approximately 1 inch (2.5 cm) from the end of the seam, stitching exactly perpendicular to the seamline as shown in the drawing on page 9. Trim. Press under the seam allowance around the upper edge.

6. Stitch the side seams in the outer bag. Overcast them, and overcast the upper edge.

7. Position the button loop at the center of the bag back upper edge, on the right side, with loop ends aligned with the bag edge. Stitch it securely in the seam allowance.

8. Fold the lower corners as for the lining, but from the right side tuck one end of the cord into each corner before stitching. Stitch the points, then stitch again in the seam allowance so the cord is securely attached. Trim.

9. Slip the lining into the bag and pin it in place across the bottom. Fold in the upper edge of the bag, matching the raw edge to that of the lining. The lining will be slightly shorter. Stitch the lining to the bag along the lining foldline.

10. Whipstitch the cord in place along the side seams.

A NUMBER OF THE PROJECTS in these chapters make use of the technique known as free machining, or free-motion stitching. The key word in the term is "free." Stitching is done with the feed dog teeth lowered so the fabric can be moved freely in any and every direction. Stitch length is regulated by the speed at which the fabric is moved in relation to the speed of the machine. In other words, the stitcher functions as the feed dogs normally would.

As you can see by the work of the designers who stitch this way (see the photos on pages 16 and 93), some wonderful effects and stitching patterns can be created. Interesting variations in stitch length, richly textured stitches, curved and wavy lines of stitching—all are made possible with this stitching method. It works well for quilting, producing especially nice patterns and surface texture. And before sewing machines learned the alphabet, this was the only way to stitch a monogram by machine.

There is nothing difficult about the technique, but it does require some practice. The secret is in gauging the speed of the machine against the speed at which you move the fabric. As with other sewing abilities, you learn with experience. Follow the guidelines below and give it a try—you'll soon be thinking up all kinds of applications for your newly acquired skill.

1. Especially at first, use a hoop for the stitching, pulling the fabric taut. Place the piece so that the fabric is against the machine bed. Later, try tearaway stabilizer instead of a hoop. A hoop isn't needed for quilting through a reasonably firm batting once you have mastered the stitching.

2. Lower the feed dog teeth.

3. Use a darning presser foot or spring embroidery foot, or use a spring needle and no presser foot at all.

A note of caution: Always remember to raise and lower the presser foot lever even though no presser foot is used. This lever also controls tension on the upper thread. Sewing with the lever up, as you know, guarantees bobbin tangles or worse. Likewise, pulling thread through the tension spring while the lever is lowered can necessitate professional tension adjustment.

4. Set the stitch width at 0 for straight stitch. The length setting is irrelevant—you will control that as you move the fabric.

5. Practice straight stitching first. Place both hands flat on the work, as close to the needle as is comfortable. Move the hoop in all directions as you sew. Keep the machine speed fairly fast; if it is too slow for the motion of the hoop, the thread will break.

6. Now practice with the stitch width set for zigzag. With greater fabric movement, you can create interesting erratic lines. Very slight movement produces satin stitch. If your machine permits adjustment of the stitch width as you sew, you can vary the width of a satin stitch line.

7. Practice writing your name with straight stitch, then with satin stitch. The first attempt may feel awkward, but the third one will be quite nice. Free!

TAPESTRY CLUTCH BAG

Interior designers usually are delighted to find homes for their samples of discontinued drapery and upholstery fabrics. Because these fabrics are intended for hard use, they are quite durable and are often finished for soil and stain resistance. In other words, they are ideal for making handbags.

Many of these fabrics offer great potential for design enhancement, responding beautifully to the addition of decorative stitching, a little beading, or couched threads that elaborate on the original theme. This designer played upon the fabric's damask pattern, using the same colors to embroider an arrangement of dainty flowers on the flap of the bag. It is lined in bright green faille.

The bag is the simplest envelope style, with an open top that folds over to keep the contents in place. Open, it measures 9-1/2 inches (24 cm) wide and 10 inches (25.5 cm) long.

MATERIALS

Upholstery fabric, medium weight: 26 by 10-1/2 inches (66 by 26.5 cm)

Lining, two pieces: 11 inches (28 cm) long and 10-1/2 inches (26.5 cm) wide

Fusible garment-weight batting: 20 by 9-1/2 inches (50.5 by 24 cm)

INSTRUCTIONS

Use 1/2 inch (1.5 cm) seam allowances except as otherwise indicated.

1. Mark off the area for embellishment on the end of the outer bag fabric that will become the flap, allowing 3 inches (8 cm) for hem and seam allowance at the end of the piece. Work embroidery, beading, couching, or whatever appeals to you.

2. Center the batting on the wrong side of the piece and fuse it according to the manufacturer's instructions.

3. Fold the piece in half crosswise, right sides together, and stitch the sides. Trim the corners; press.

4. With right sides together, stitch the lining sections along the two 11-inch (28-cm) sides and across one shorter side, leaving a 4-inch (10-cm) opening on the latter for turning. Trim corners; press.

5. Place the lining inside the bag, right sides together and raw edges aligned. Stitch; turn through the opening.

Designer: NELL PAULK

FLORAL BAG

Free-motion stitching through three fabric layers adds wonderful surface texture to the print fabric. The stitching is worked in threads to match the print colors and repeats the pattern of the print. For the closure, a knotted fabric strip simply wraps around the large ornamental button.

The bag is 6 inches (15 cm) wide and 7 inches (18 cm) long. The strap length is 42 inches (106.5 cm).

MATERIALS

Fabric for outer bag: a rectangle 7-3/4 by 21 inches (19.5 by 53 cm)

Lining fabric, the same size as outer fabric piece

Garment-weight batting or cotton flannel, the size of the outer fabric piece

Fabric for edge binding, button loop, and strap: to match or complement the outer bag fabric

A large button

Designer: KAREN SWING

CONSTRUCTION

The fabric dimensions given above are slightly larger than the size needed because dense stitching will draw them up slightly. The piece will be trimmed to size after the layers are stitched. Allow for this when planning a design.

Stitching the layers

Please read about free-motion stitching, page 14.

1. Layer the fabric rectangles, the outer fabric and lining right side out with the batting between. Pin baste.

2. To stabilize the fabric for stitching, spray-starch one side of the piece, allow it to dry, then starch the other side.

3. Using the free-motion stitching technique, stitch over the entire piece to hold the layers together. Use thread colors to highlight or contrast with your fabric colors.

4. When the stitching is finished, trim the piece to 7 by 21 inches (18 by 53.5 cm).

Assembly

1. With right sides together, fold the lower edge of the bag upward by 7-1/2 inches (19 cm). Stitch the sides, using 1/4 inch (.7 cm) seam allowance. Overcast the seam allowances neatly.

2. With the bag wrong side out, fold each lower corner to create a point at the lower end of the seam. Stitch across the point approximately 1 inch (2.5 cm) from the end of the seam, stitching exactly perpendicular to the seamline as shown in the drawing on page 9. This will give the bag depth.

3. Trim the sides of the flap so they are slightly narrower than the finished front of the bag (see the illustration on page 11). Round the corners slightly at the upper edges of the opening. Round the corners of the flap.

4. Serge or overcast all raw edges.

Edge binding and finishing

1. For the edge binding, cut a strip 1-1/2 inches (4 cm) wide and approximately 24 inches (61 cm) long. strap. For smooth application, cut it on the bias.

2. Cut the strap on the lengthwise fabric grain, 1-1/2 inches (4 cm) wide and 43 inches (109 cm) long, or the desired length.

3. Cut the button strip 1-1/2 inches (4 cm) wide and 6 inches (16 cm) long (it can be shortened later).

4. For the strap, sew the long edges of the strip, right sides together, using 1/4 inch (.7 cm) seam allowance. Turn and press. Alternatively, press the strip in half, right side out. Fold the raw edges in to the center; press. Stitch along both long edges.

5. Stitch the button loop in the same way. Position one end at the center of the flap edge on the right side.

6. On the bag right side, align the strap ends with the edge of the bag at the side seamlines.

7. Beginning on the front, stitch the binding strip to the bag, right sides together and edges aligned, using 3/8 inch (1 cm) seam allowance. At the flap/front corners, ease the fabric and clip into the seam allowances as necessary. Fold under the overlapping end. Press binding toward the seam allowances.

8. Fold under the raw edge of the strip so the fold just covers the previous stitching line and stitch by hand.

9. Sew the button on the bag front. If a shank button is not used, make a long thread shank for the button to accommodate the fabric strip. Adjust the length of the button strip if necessary and knot the end.

Leather Pouch

A variation on the clutch style, this small bag has a gusset between front and back. The uneven edges of the soft garment-weight leather supplied the design inspiration. The flap is a separate piece, sewn to the upper back edge with two strap carriers incorporated into the seam. Narrow leather strips were braided together for the strap. The horn netsuke that ornaments the flap was a souvenir of a memorable trip to Japan. The bag measures approximately 6 by 8 inches (15 by 20 cm).

Since every piece of leather is different, the instructions below will not produce an exact duplicate of the bag shown. That's the beauty of leather!

Materials and Tools

Garment-weight leather, approximately 4 sq. feet (.37 sq. m)

An interesting ornament or button for the flap

Glue stick

Mallet: rubber, rawhide, or wood

Instructions

Before you begin, please read the tips on working with leather, opposite.

Cutting

1. Make a paper pattern for the front and back. Cut a rectangle the desired size, then fold it lengthwise and round the two lower corners. Cut from the leather.

2. Cut a gusset strip the total length of the bag sides and bottom and approximately 1-1/2 inches (4 cm) wide. Piece the strip if necessary.

3. For the flap, take advantage of an interesting edge of the leather. Cut one straight edge the width of the bag upper edge. The flap length should approximately equal the bag length.

4. Cut a pocket the shape of the bag front/back, but smaller, adding hem allowance across the top.

5. For the strap carriers, cut two pieces approximately 2 inches (5 cm) long and 1-1/2 inches (4 cm) wide. Fold each in half across, then taper the sides from the edges toward the fold, so the piece is approximately 1 inch (2.5 cm) across the fold. Glue-baste the ends together.

Strap

Determine the desired length of the strap, allowing a few extra inches to tie the ends. Cut strips approximately 1/8 inch (3 mm) wide and braid three together to the length needed. The strips need not be final strap length; when one is used up, just work in another. The protruding ends will give it character.

Designer: **Liz Spear**

Construction

1. Fold the hem across the top of the pocket and tap the fold with the mallet. Stitch. Place the pocket, right side up, on the wrong side of the bag back. Stitch approximately 1/8 inch (3 mm) from the edge.

2. Position the strap carriers on the right side of the bag back, ends aligned with the upper edge, approximately 1/2 inch (1.5 cm) from each side. Glue baste.

3. Stitch the flap to the bag back, right sides together, using 1/4 inch (.7 cm) seam allowance. Smooth the seam allowances toward the bag and tap with the mallet.

4. Stitch the gusset, right sides together, to one bag section then the other, using 1/4 inch (.7 mm) seam allowance. Clip as necessary around the curves. Trim. Tap the seam allowances toward the gusset. Topstitch, if desired, close to the seam-line.

Finishing

1. Thread the strap through the carriers and knot the ends together.

2. An ornament at the lower edge of the flap is not merely decorative—its weight helps keep the flap in place. For this one, two small holes were made near the edge of the flap. Narrow strips of leather were threaded through the holes and through the ornament, then tied.

WORKING WITH LEATHER

Sewing Garment-weight leather or suede on a home sewing machine is not the least bit difficult. In fact, the "fabric" is probably much easier to work with than many materials you have used. Note the tips offered below, and your first leather project will please you greatly.

Leather is sold by the square foot rather than the linear yard (meter), so you'll need to convert yardage requirements to square feet. Generally, figure 11 square feet (1.15 square m) of leather or suede equals 1 yard (1 m) of 45-inch (115-cm) fabric. Add 15 percent for irregularly shaped skins.

1. It is a good idea to take the pattern pieces along with you when you shop to be sure of buying a skin of adequate size for the project. Choose skins designated as "garment weight." These weigh between 1 and 2-1/2 ounces (29 and 71 g) per square foot (929 square cm).

2. The "lengthwise grainline" direction on a skin is parallel to the animal's backbone. Major pieces should be cut in this direction. For suede, lay out pieces as for napped fabric.

3. Cut out the pieces singly. Do not cut on a fold.

4. Use small binder clips instead of pins to secure the pieces for sewing. Glue stick, applied in the seam allowance, is another good choice.

5. Use a machine needle designated for leather. The point is chisel-shaped to make a minute, self-healing slit in the skin with each stitch rather than piercing a hole. Use a size appropriate for the project.

6. Sew with polyester or cotton-wrapped polyester thread.

7. Use a teflon foot. An even-feed foot also works well.

8. For handwork, use a glover's needle (it has a triangular tip) in the smallest size that will penetrate the hide.

9. The ideal pressing method is to finger press seams open and tap with a rawhide, wood, or rubber mallet. The high heat of an iron can damage leather or suede. Glue or stitch seam allowances to secure them.

10. Sew-in interfacing should be used, the weight consistent with the project requirements. Always test a sample.

11. Leather and suede do not ravel, so edge finishing is not necessary. Beveling edges gives a flatter finish.

12. Hems may be stitched or glued in place with a permanent contact cement.

RUG-PATTERNED BAG

The design of a magnificent old Caucasian rug translates easily into needlepoint. The lines of the pattern inspired the bag shape, its pointed flap neatly edged in the design colors.

The bag was worked all in basketweave stitch with two strands of Persian yarn. The solid-colored area under the flap provides a discreet place in which to stitch the designer's initials. Strands of the yarn were braided together then knotted and stitched in place to make a quick and colorful strap.

The texture of denim works well for a lining. The designer took advantage of the fabric's attractive selvage along the front of the bag.

If needlepoint is not among your interests, what about a trade with a friend who is adept at needlepoint but cannot sew? The design of the bag itself would work just as well with other heavy fabrics. An old tapestry, perhaps found at a flea market and too badly worn for display, might yield an undamaged section that would make a beautiful bag.

The finished bag is 7-1/2 inches (19 cm) square.

Designer: NELL PAULK

Materials

Bargello canvas: 13 count, 8-1/2 by 21-3/4 inches (21.5 by 55 cm)

Persian yarn: red, dark blue, medium blue, gold

Fabric for lining: 8-1/2 by 23-3/4 inches (21.5 by 57.5 cm)

A large snap

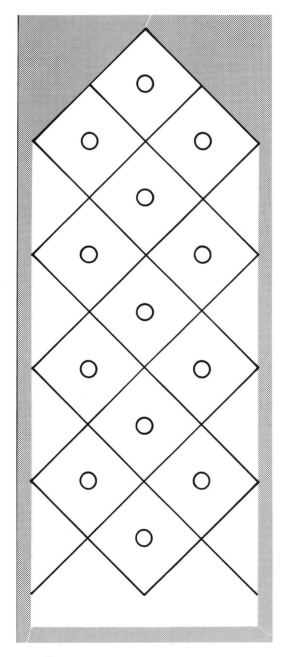

OMIT STITCHING IN THE SHADED AREA.

Instructions

Use the photos as a guide for the pattern and colors.

The needlepoint

1. Leave unstitched a 1-inch (2.5-cm) margin of canvas at one short end and a 1/2-inch (1.3-cm) margin at the remaining short end and along both long edges, as indicated by the diagram.

2. Mark the center point of the stitching area at the end of the canvas with the narrower margin. To set up the design, measure 3 inches (7.5 cm) from the point and work a line of basketweave stitches to the other side. Repeat, working the other direction from the point.

3. Measure and work the remaining diagonal lines, then fill in the diamonds. If you wish, add a monogram on the unpatterned area (the bag front).

4. When the stitching is complete, turn under and steam press the margins on the two long edges and the pointed flap.

Construction

1. On the lining, press under the seam allowances on the two long edges and the flap, fitting to the needle-

point. Position the needlepoint and lining with wrong sides together. Edgestitch together around the three sides with short stitches.

2. Fold a double hem in the remaining lining edge, folding it to cover the raw edge of the canvas. Stitch the hem to the canvas, close to the fold. Stitch again near the upper edge.

3. Fold the piece, right side out, 6-1/2 inches (16.5 cm) from the straight edge to form the envelope. Sew the side seams, stitching close to the edge. Steam press the piece and allow it to dry.

Finishing

1. Make two strap sections. Choose three yarn colors, and braid together three strand of each to a length of 24 inches (61 cm), or the length desired. Tie an overhand knot at each end.

2. Sew one strap end to the inner flap fold on each side. Stitch securely to the lining, just catching the canvas. Tie the free ends together.

3. Stitch one snap section approximately 2-1/2 inches from the point, stitching through the lining and invisibly into the canvas. Stitch the other section to the bag front through all thicknesses.

CHAPTER 2

SHOULDER BAGS

Although many of the bags described in other chapters are technically shoulder bags—they have long straps—the styles shown here are larger bags, meant to carry a good bit of stuff as often we do. When you make a working bag like one of

these, choose fabric that is durable and that will bear up under the weight. Sew seams securely. French seams, reinforced seams, and overcast seams are some options. If you use a serger, use the four-thread stitch, or sew the seam with a machine straight stitch and use the serger for overcasting. Attach handles and straps securely, too, with extra rows of stitching.

23

Geometric Play

Colorful fabrics, pieced in the Seminole style, transform a simple bag design into a work of art. Playing with colors and designs for the patchwork is great fun! If you haven't tried this technique, a useful bag like this provides a good reason to start.

This bag is lined and piped with solid black cotton to set off the design. A patchwork pocket on the lining offers one more opportunity to experiment.

Materials

Assorted fabrics for piecing: all-cotton quilting fabrics work well.

Lining fabric, 1 yard (1 m)

A strip of lightweight fusible interfacing for the strap

Piping cord, 1-1/4 yards (1.15 m)

Decorative plastic rings, 2 inches (5 cm) in diameter

Designer: **dj** BENNETT

INSTRUCTIONS

The finished bag measures 13 by 15 inches (33 by 86 cm), and it could easily be made larger or smaller. The finished strap is 34 inches (36 cm) long.

Piecing

A number of good books and magazine articles have been written about Seminole piecing. If this bag piques your interest, there are hundreds of design ideas waiting to be tried. The basic procedure is very simple, but cutting and stitching must be done with precision.

The simplest design is a pattern of squares. Cut fabric strips of the same width in assorted colors. Join them along the long edges, pressing the seam allowances to one side as you go. When the piece is approximately square, cut it, perpendicular to the stitching lines, into strips the same width as the original strips. Reassemble the square, offsetting the colors. Because reassembling the strips means some waste at the ends of each, you will always want to start with a piece somewhat larger than the finished size you will need.

When you have mastered the checkered pattern, try some variations. Make up the block with strips of varying widths, or reassemble the cut block on the diagonal. Use the bag in the photo to inspire your own patterns.

Make finished blocks for the bag front and back, slightly larger than the lining dimensions, below. Trim them to the size of the lining. Piece a strip for the strap, trimmed to the size of the strap lining. Make another piece, if you wish, for a lining pocket—7 by 5 inches (18 by 13 cm) is a good size.

Cutting

1. Cut two pieces of lining for the bag front and back, 14 by 16 inches (36 by 41 cm).

2. Cut one strap lining, 39 by 2-1/4 inches (99 by 5.5 cm), piecing if necessary.

3. Cut pocket lining the size of the patchwork.

4. For ring attachment loops, cut two pieces of lining or patchwork fabric, 2 inches (5 cm) square.

5. Cut fusible interfacing 39 by 1-3/4 inches (99 by 4.5 cm).

6. For piping, cut bias strips approximately 1-1/2 inches (4 cm) wide and piece them to a length of 46 inches (117 cm).

Construction

Seam allowances are 1/2 inch (1.5 cm) unless otherwise noted.

1. Trim the finished patchwork pieces to the size of the corresponding lining pieces.

2. Wrap the bias strip around the piping cord and stitch close to the cord with a zipper or cording foot.

3. Pin the piping to the right side of one bag section with the piping stitching line on the bag seamline. At corners, clip into the piping seam allowance almost to the stitching so that the piping lies flat. Stitch from the piping side, on the piping stitching line.

4. Pin this piece to the other bag section and stitch, again on the previous stitching line.

5. At the ends, clip away the cord from the piping to the seamline.

6. Sew the pocket lining to the pocket, right sides together, leaving an opening for turning. Turn right side out and press. Topstitch, if desired, across the top edge.

7. Topstitch the pocket to the right side of one lining section.

8. Stitch the lining sections together, leaving a fairly large opening on the bottom for turning.

9. Fold each of the small squares in half, and press. Fold the raw edges in to the center crease, press, and topstitch along both edges.

10. Fold each strip in half over a plastic ring and pin to the bag right side at the seamline, ends aligned with the edge of the bag.

11. With the bag and the lining wrong side out, place the lining in the bag, matching the upper edges. Stitch, press, and turn through the opening. Topstitch around the upper edge. Close the opening.

12. Fuse interfacing to the strap lining, centering it on the strip.

13. Using 1/4 inch (.5 cm) seam allowance, stitch the strap to its lining with right sides together. Turn. Press ends to the inside. Topstitch around all edges.

14. Fold approximately 2 inches (5 cm) of each strap end through a plastic ring and stitch it securely in place.

Teardrop Bag

Designer: **Lori Kerr**

This wonderfully practical bag is spacious enough to accommodate all the gear your day requires. Whether it's worn to the back or to the front, the shape provides for more comfortable weight distribution so you don't end the day with one sagging shoulder.

As you can see by the variations shown on the following pages, the basic bag is a perfect candidate for interesting fabric combinations and for embellishments of every description. We've shown it first in natural cotton duck so the construction details will be clearly visible, but can you picture it in heavy raw silk? How about one of the colorfully printed water-repellent fabrics made for outdoor furniture covering? A miniature rendition of the design makes an attractive evening bag; it's shown on page 82.

The bag has a wide strap for wearing comfort. Its length can be made adjustable with the addition of extra buttonholes at the end of the upper strap section.

This model has a large pocket on each side, the openings covered by flaps and topped with decorative bands. The pocket design can easily be altered to suit your own needs. It could be divided vertically by rows of stitching, or buttons might be added to the flaps. It would be easy, too, to add another pocket above, sewing it into the side seams in the same way. Our model is not lined—the seams are serged—but adding a lining takes little extra time, and allows for the addition of more pockets still.

The finished bag is 11 inches (28 cm) across the widest point, 20 inches (50.5 cm) high, and 6-1/2 inches (16.5 cm) deep at the bottom.

MATERIALS

Fabric: medium to heavy weight, approximately 1 yard (1 m), 54 to 60 inches (137 to 152 cm) wide, or 1-1/2 yards (1.4 m) at 45 inches (115 cm). If you make design changes, additional fabric may be needed.

Zipper: a sturdy one, 15 inches (38 cm) long

One button, approximately 1 inch (2.5 cm) diameter

INSTRUCTIONS

Seam allowances are 3/8 inch (1 cm) except where otherwise noted.

Cutting

1. Enlarge the pattern pieces and from fabric cut two front/back sections, one side gusset, and four pocket flaps.

2. Cut two pockets from the lower front/back pattern as indicated.

3. Cut two pocket flap trim strips on the fabric cross-grain, 11 inches (28 cm) wide and 3 inches (8 cm) long.

4. Cut two zipper gusset sections on the lengthwise grain, 19-3/8 inches (49 cm) long and 3-3/8 inches (8.5 cm) wide.

5. Cut one upper strap on the lengthwise grain, 30 inches (76 cm) long and 9 inches (23 cm) wide.

6. Cut one lower strap on the lengthwise grain, 16 1/2 inches (42 cm) long and 9 inches (23 cm) wide.

7. For the strap connector loop, cut a lengthwise strip 8-1/2 inches (21.5 cm) long and 2 inches (5 cm) wide.

Pockets and flaps

1. Place two pocket flap sections with right sides together. Stitch the ends and curved edge, leaving the long straight edge open. Trim, turn right side out, and press. Topstitch around the seamed edge. Make the second flap the same way.

2. Hem the upper straight edge of each pocket with a 1/2-inch (1.5-cm) double hem. Place a pocket right side up on the right side of the bag front and back sections, aligning the curved edges. Baste.

3. Position the flaps with the unfinished edges at the placement lines. Baste them in place along the upper seamlines.

4. On the flap trim strips, fold under each raw edge 3/4 inch (2 cm), and press. Pin a strip over each pocket flap with the fold along the flap upper seamline. Topstitch the strip in place along both long edges.

Install the zipper

1. Fold each zipper gusset piece in half lengthwise, right side out, and press the fold.

2. Open the pieces out, place them with right sides together. Machine baste together along the crease

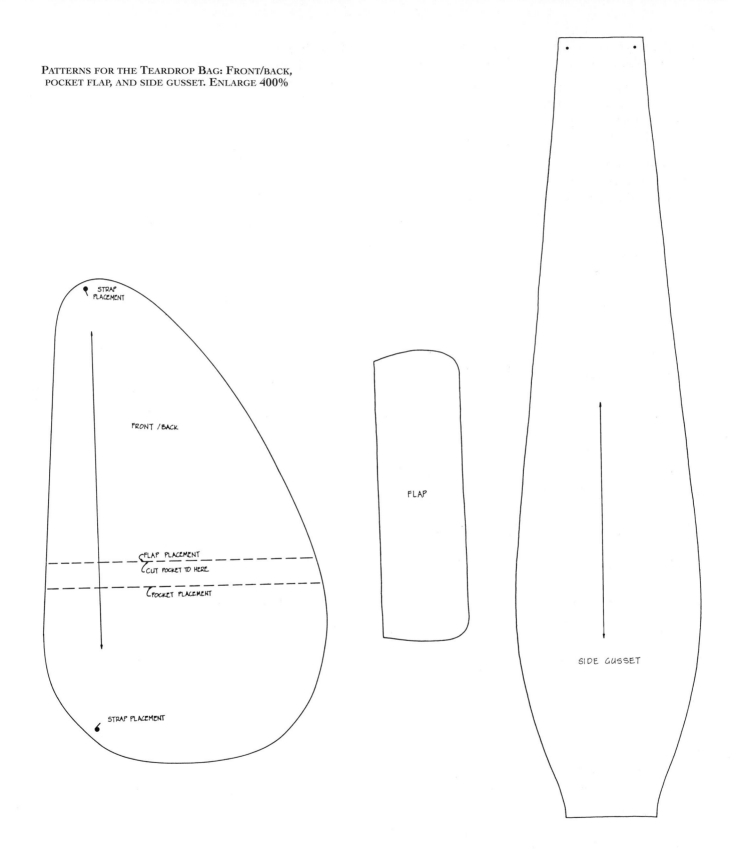

PATTERNS FOR THE TEARDROP BAG: FRONT/BACK,
POCKET FLAP, AND SIDE GUSSET. ENLARGE 400%

STRAP
PLACEMENT

FRONT /BACK

FLAP PLACEMENT

CUT POCKET TO HERE

POCKET PLACEMENT

STRAP PLACEMENT

FLAP

SIDE GUSSET

line, stitching both ends of the seam at regular stitch length for about 2 inches (5 cm). Press open, as before.

3. Stitch the zipper into the basted section of the seam, following package instructions for a centered zipper. For security, stitch again just outside the first stitching lines and stitch across the ends.

Make the straps

1. Press the upper and lower strap sections in half lengthwise, right side out. Fold the raw edges in to the center crease; press. Stitch each long edge with two rows of topstitching.

2. Clean finish one end of the upper strap. Work three buttonholes, centering them on the strap and with the center of the lower one 5 inches (13 cm) from the finished end of the strap.

3. Sew the button onto the "wrong" side of the strap, approximately 1 inch (2.5 cm) from the finished end.

4. Press the strap connector strip as you did the straps. Topstitch along the long edges.

5. Overlap the ends by 1/4 inch (.5 cm) to form a loop. Stitch with a zigzag stitch, overcasting the raw ends.

6. Slip the loop over the lower strap. Fold the strap in half and baste the strap together. With the loop at the strap fold, stitch two lines of stitching across the doubled strap to keep the loop in place.

Assembling the bag

1. With both pieces right side up, pin the unfinished end of the upper strap to the upper end of the zipper gusset. With right sides together, pin the upper end of the side gusset piece to the other two pieces, so that the strap is sandwiched between the two gusset sections and all raw edges are aligned. Stitch, then stitch again in the seam allowance and/or overcast.

2. Sandwich the end of the lower strap between the gusset sections in the same way; stitch.

3. Pin and stitch one front or back section in place, easing as necessary around the curves. Take care to keep the straps out of the way. Clip the seam allowances around the curves. Finish the seam as above.

4. Open the zipper a little, and pin and stitch the other front/back piece in the same way. Open the zipper fully to turn the bag right side out.

A lined bag

To add a lining, cut the front, back, and gusset pieces by the pattern. Add pockets if you wish. Press the zipper gusset pieces as for the bag, but don't stitch them together. Trim away approximately 1/4 inch (.5 cm) from the long raw edges of each piece so that when the bag is put together the folds will just cover the edges of the zipper tape. Leave 1/2 inch (1 cm) between these pieces when they are joined to the side gusset.

Assemble the lining as the bag. Put it in place. Stitch to the bag around the front/back/gusset seams, stitching from the outside in the ditch formed by the seam. Whipstitch the folded edges of the zipper gusset to the zipper tape.

Adorned with Appliqué

Woodland creatures make a colorful statement on this variation. The motifs are cut from a commercially printed fabric. Just think of the possibilities! The pockets feature hook and loop tape fasteners, stitched in place before the pockets and flaps were basted to the bag front and back.

Instructions

1. Cut out the bag pieces as for the basic bag, page 27.

2. For the appliqué, back the printed fabric piece with paper-backed fusible web, following the manufacturer's instructions. Then cut out the individual motifs. Position them on the bag pieces, keeping clear of the seam allowances, and fuse them in place.

3. For stitching, use thread in a contrasting color, or try a decorative thread if you wish. Stitch around each motif several times and use additional stitching to highlight tiny details.

4. Assemble the bag as for the basic design.

Designer: **Lori Kerr**

MIXED PATTERNS

It's always fun to play with fabric combinations, experimenting with several prints, colliding colors, or interesting textures. Sometimes, as in this case, it's the combination that inspires embellishment. For this designer, the fabric colors invoked delicious thoughts of watermelon, so she used fabric paint to add just a few seeds for accent. Solid-colored corded piping highlights the seamlines, and (clever designer!) creates a visual distraction along the seams where it isn't possible to match the checked pattern.

INSTRUCTIONS

1. Choose complementary fabrics according to your whim, and cut the bag pieces from the pattern and instructions on pages 27-29. Note that the pocket for this bag is cut on the bias.

2. You will need approximately 3 yards (2.75 m) of 1/8-inch (3-mm) piping cord. Cut bias fabric strips approximately 1-1/2 inches (4 cm) wide and piece them to the needed length. Fold the strip around the cord and stitch close to the cord with a zipper foot.

3. Add the pockets and flaps to the bag front and back sections as described on page 27. Stitch the piping to the right side of the bag front and back, matching the piping stitching line to the bag seamline. Where the end of the piping meets the beginning, cut the end approximately 1/2 inch (1 cm) past the joining point. Clip out that length of cord, clip the stitching, and turn the ends inside so the fold just covers the beginning. Whipstitch in place.

4. Complete the bag assembly as described previously.

Design adaptation: TRACY MUNN

PATCHWORK LEATHER TEARDROP BAG

Scraps of soft, colorful leather were pieced to create a stunning version of the basic shoulder bag. A machine featherstitch was used for the piecing, adding stitching interest and strengthening the seams at the same time. Pocket flaps were eliminated and the natural edge of the leather was used for the upper pocket edge.

INSTRUCTIONS

For more information about sewing with leather, read the tips on page 19. The bag is constructed as described on pages 27-30, but with a few differences.

1. Use the pattern as a guide for piecing scraps for the bag front and back. So that the pieces will abut precisely, stack the two pieces that will join, then cut through both at the same time. Use a single piece of leather for the side gusset.

2. To prevent the pocket gaping, stitch the pocket to the bag front/back along the pocket edge approximately 2 inches (5 cm) in from each side seam.

3. Use a heavier zipper, perhaps one of the decorative types. Choose a heavier piece of leather for the zipper gusset pieces, and use just a single thickness. On the bag shown, the zipper teeth are exposed, so approximately 1/4 inch (.5 cm) was trimmed from one long edge of each piece. This necessitated adding a small piece of leather at each end of the zipper, stitching it so it overlaps the ends of the gusset pieces. Where it joins the side gusset, it is stitched with right sides together as for the fabric bags.

4. For the straps, cut the strips 4-1/2 inches (11 cm) wide. Fold them in half and topstitch. Trim the raw edges evenly after stitching, if necessary. Cut the strip for the connecting loop 1 inch (2.5 cm) wide and construct it the same way.

5. Eliminate the buttonholes and button. Simply tie the upper strap around the connecting loop as shown in the photo.

6. Do add a lining; it not only will cover all those piecing seams, but will strengthen the bag as well.

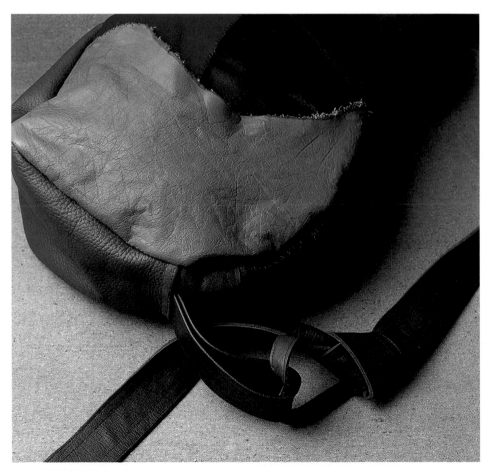

Designer: LORI KERR

Designer: **SANDY SCRIVANO**

SUEDE-LINED LEATHER BAG

Sewing leather or suede with a standard sewing machine is a snap when you use leather of an appropriate weight and follow the guidelines on page 19. If you can't find garment leather in your area, check with the mail order sources that advertise in sewing magazines.

A single piece of leather makes up the back, bottom, and front of the bag. Contrasting side gussets give the bag its depth and provide for secure attachment of the strap. The flap, attached at the upper back edge, is layered of pieces of both leathers, cut from the edges of the skins. Not only is the finish uniquely decorative, but it puts to good use leather pieces that might otherwise end up in the scrap box. To strengthen these points, the flap edges and the bag opening are bound with leather strips.

The strap is a doubled strip of leather, seamed along one side and interfaced with grosgrain ribbon to prevent stretching. The lining is soft pigskin, almost the color of the outer bag. It is customized with pockets to accommodate the designer's essentials, in this case two pairs of glasses, mobile phone (she is the mother of teenagers), keys, lipstick, and pens and pencils.

The bag measures 12-1/2 inches (31.5 cm) high, 12 inches (30.5 cm) wide, and 2 inches (5 cm) deep. The strap is 1 inch (2.5 cm) wide and 50 inches (127 cm) long, measured from the top of the bag. It is a good idea to make paper pattern pieces from the cutting dimensions below and take them with you when you shop.

MATERIALS AND TOOLS

Bag outer shell and strap: 2-1/2 ounce (71 g) leather, 13 sq. feet (1.2 sq. m) total, one color or a combination of colors,

Lining: pigsuede, 1 ounce (29 g), 10 sq. feet (.93 sq. m). Amount may vary depending upon your own pocket designs.

Organza for interfacing: 1 sq. foot (929 sq. cm)

Grosgrain ribbon: 1-2/3 yards (1.55 m), 1 inch (2.5 cm) wide

Sewing thread: cotton-wrapped polyester or 100 percent polyester

Optional: a special button or ornament for the flap

Glue stick

Permanent contact cement

Mallet: rubber, rawhide, or wood

INSTRUCTIONS

Please read the tips for sewing with leather on page 19. Seam allowances are 5/8 inch (1.5 cm) except as noted. Use the clamps, not pins, to hold seams for stitching. Glue baste as necessary. For permanent gluing, use contact cement. Do not backstitch seam ends, but pull the threads to the wrong side and tie in a square knot.

Cutting

Lay out the pattern pieces to plan placement before cutting.

1. For the bag outer shell, cut one piece 26 by 13-5/8 inches (66 by 34.5 cm).

2. Cut lining the same size as the outer shell.

3. Cut two side gussets from outer shell leather and two for lining, 13 by 3-1/4 inches (33 by 8.25 cm). At one end (the lower end) of each piece, round the corners slightly.

4. Cut strips 3-3/4 inches (9.5 cm) wide to piece for the strap. Add to the desired finished length of the strap 6 inches (16 cm) for the attached ends. For piecing, add seam allowance at each end of each strip and plan to sew piecing seams on the diagonal.

5. To cover the strap ends, cut two pieces 3-1/2 inches (9 cm) square.

6. From the organza, cut one piece 12 inches (30.5 cm)

by 2 inches (5 cm). Cut two pieces 3-1/2 inches (9 cm) square.

7. Cut pieces for the flap 13-1/2 inches (34 cm) wide. On the bag shown, the under layer of the flap (the longer layer) is approximately 11 inches (28 cm) long and the short upper layer is approximately 6 inches (15 cm). On the model, two additional strips cut from the edges of the two skins are sandwiched between. These do not extend into the flap seam, but are just a few inches long.

8. To cover the flap seam at the upper back of the bag, cut another strip from the edge of the skin used for the main part of the bag. It should be 13-1/2 inches (34 cm) wide and approximately 2-1/2 to 4 inches (6.5 to 10 cm) long, the rough edge along the width.

9. Cut two strips for flap edge binding, each 1-5/8 inches (4 cm) wide and the length of the upper flap layer plus 1/2 inch (1.5 cm) seam allowance.

10. Cut binding strip for the bag upper edge, 1-5/8 inches (4 cm) wide and 36 inches (91 cm) long.

11. From lining skin, cut pocket pieces the desired size and shape. Allow approximately 3/8 inch (1 cm) for side and bottom seams, and allow 1-1/2-inch (4-cm) hems at the tops. For pocket ideas, see page 5.

Strap

1. Piece the strap sections as necessary, stitching these seams on the diagonal for strength. Open the seam allowances and tap them smooth with the mallet.

2. Glue-baste the ribbon to the wrong side of the strap, one edge of the ribbon aligned with an edge of the strap.

3. Fold along the inner edge of the ribbon and tap the fold with the mallet. Glue-baste to secure the fold.

4. Along the uninterfaced edge, fold in the seam allowance. Tap along the fold.

5. Fold the strap lengthwise so the two folded edges are aligned. Tap the folds. Topstitch 1/8 inch (3 mm) from each long edge.

Side gussets

1. Glue-baste an interfacing square to the wrong side of each outer gusset piece at the upper edge.

2. Position a strap end, right side up, on the right side of one gusset, the strap end 3 inches (7.5 cm) below the upper edge of the gusset. Glue the lower 2 inches (5 cm) of the strap in place. Stitch around the glued area.

3. With right sides together, place strap cover piece 1-5/8 inches (4 cm) from the upper edge. Stitch in place across the gusset and strap.

4. Fold the flap down, and tap the seam. Glue-baste it in place in the side seam allowances. Topstitch across the lower edge.

Joining gussets and body

1. Fit a gusset section to each long edge of the bag, right sides together, and hold with clamps. Clip and notch around bottom curves as necessary. Stitch.

2. Smooth the seam allowances toward the gussets. Topstitch around the gussets close to the seamlines. Trim seam allowances.

Flap and flap cover

1. Layer the flap sections, aligning the back edges (those opposite the rough edges). Glue-baste together in the back seam allowance. Glue-baste the layers on the flap front, leaving some of the rough edges free. To secure the layers, topstitch through all layers, following the lines of the upper layer edge.

2. Bind the sides of the flap. Plan the binding strips to extend from the back edge of the flap to the end of the upper flap layer, or as looks best with your design. With right sides together, sew a binding strip along each edge, using 1/4 inch (.7 cm) seam allowance. Smooth the seam allowances toward the binding. Wrap the binding around the seam allowances and hold with clamps. From the right side, topstitch in the ditch through all layers. Trim close to the stitching.

3. Glue-baste an interfacing strip across the wrong side of the bag back, 3/4 inch (2 cm) below the upper edge.

4. On the flap seam cover, fold under the seam allowances at the sides. Tap, then glue them.

5. Position the straight end of the flap 1-5/8 inches (4 cm) below the edge of bag back, underside of the flap to the bag right side. Glue-baste along the seam allowance.

6. With right sides together, place the flap cover over the flap, aligning the edges. Stitch 5/8 inch (1.5 cm) from the edge and again at 3/8 inch (1 cm).

7. Fold flap cover down over the seam. Tap, and glue into position.

Lining

1. Construct pockets as desired and apply them to the lining, keeping clear of the seam allowances. To stitch them, place the pocket wrong side to the right side of the lining. Stitch close to the edge, then again 1/4 inch (.5 cm) inside the first stitching line.

2. Join side gussets and body of the lining as for the outer shell. This time, smooth the seam allowances toward the body of the bag. Topstitch close to the seams.

Finishing

1. Slip the lining into the bag, matching side seams and top edges.

2. Place the binding strip and bag with right sides together, edges aligned at the top of the bag. Overlap the binding ends by 5/8 inch (1.5 cm). Stitch with 1/4 inch (.7 cm) seam allowance.

3. Wrap the binding to the inside around the seam allowances. Hold in position with binder clips. From the right side, topstitch in the ditch. Trim close to the seam.

4. If you wish, glue or stitch an ornament to the front flap.

Shaggy Appliqué Bag

This bag is so quick to make—and such fun to embellish—that you'll find yourself doing them by the half-dozen. In a medium size, it's an indestructible school bag for the kids. A larger version is handy to keep in the car for grocery shopping. It can be embroidered, personalized with a monogram, or supplied with any appliqué that comes to mind.

The fabric is durable cotton canvas, pre-washed and frayed. We have used a hook and loop tape closure at the top, but you could easily substitute a large whimsical button with a crocheted or fabric loop stitched into the hem.

This bag is 13 inches (33 cm) wide and 10-1/2 inches (26.5 cm) high. The strap is 2 inches (5 cm) wide, 33 inches (84 cm) long. Adjust the fabric yardage if you alter the size.

MATERIALS
Fabric for bag: cotton canvas or duck, 1/2 yard (.5 m)

Paper-backed fusible web

Fabric scraps for appliqué

Decorative thread for appliqué

Hook and loop tape or button

INSTRUCTIONS
Machine wash and dry the fabric to preshrink it.

Cutting
1. The bag is cut with the length on the fabric crossgrain (it frays better this way). Cut one piece 13 inches (33 cm) long and 25 inches (63.5 cm) wide.

2. Cut one strap, also on the crossgrain, 6 inches (15 cm) wide and 35 inches (89 cm) long.

Appliqué
1. Enlarge the appliqué pattern, or design your own motif.

2. Fuse web to the wrong side of the fabric pieces according to the manufacturer's instructions.

3. Trace the motifs on the paper backing and cut out the shapes.

4. Press the pieces to the front half of the bag, planning for a 2-inch (5-cm) hem allowance at the top.

5. Stitch the shapes in place. On the model, we used rayon thread and several rows of straight stitch, adding leaf veins with the stitching.

Construction
1. Fold the strap in thirds, right side out. Press.

2. Stitch 1/2 inch (1.5 cm) from the overlapping raw edge. Stitch again, 1/2 inch (1.5 cm) from the folded edge.

3. Pull threads along the exposed edge to make a fringe.

4. Hem the upper edges of the bag. Fold under 2 inches (5 cm) at each short end of the bag; press. Fold the raw edge in to the crease. Press, and stitch close to the fold. Stitch again approximately 1/4 inch (.7 cm) from the edge. If a button loop will be added, position it at the center of the bag back and stitch the ends securely into the hem.

5. For a hook and loop tape closure, stitch one section of the tape to each hemmed edge.

6. Fold the piece in half, right side out, with the hemmed edges together. Slip 1 inch (2.5 cm) of each strap end between the hemmed edges of the bag so that the frayed edges of the strap align with the sides of the bag.

7. Sew the sides of the bag, stitching 1/2 inch (1.5 cm) from the edges and again approximately 1 inch (2.5 cm) in. Reinforce over each strap end by stitching an X.

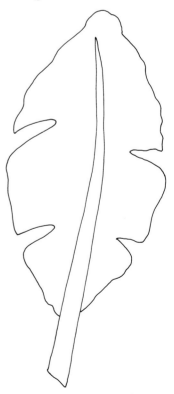

APPLIQUÉ MOTIF. ENLARGE 143%.

Designer: LORI KERR

Raffia Hobo Bag

Designer: JUDI ALWEIL

A quintessential summer bag, crocheted of rayon raffia yarn, takes you from work to a garden party or the beach. It's a good companion for touring and shopping, too.

The model features stripes in sunny blossom colors, but your own can as easily be made in a solid go-with-everything color or a bright shade to accent summer neutrals. We've added a bunch of beaded grapes as a focal point. You might choose an antique pin, a miniature doll, a lucky charm, or a handmade tassel to personalize your design.

The bag measures 11 inches (28 cm) in width and is 26 inches (66 cm) long, strap included.

MATERIALS

Rayon raffia yarn, 72-yard (66-m) skeins: 4 of main color (MC) and one each of orange (A), purple (B), and hot pink (C)

Crochet hook, U.S. size F

Magnetic snap

Ornament

INSTRUCTIONS

Crochet abbreviations are explained on page 59.
Gauge: 4 sc = 1 inch (2.5 cm).

Work the stripe pattern as follows:

Base	MC
3 rows	MC
6 rows	A
2 rows	MC
2 rows	B
2 rows	MC
6 rows	C
2 rows	MC
2 rows	B
2 rows	MC
6 rows	A

Base

Ch 4. Sl st in first ch from hook to form ring.

Row 1: sc in ring 6 times. Do not join on any of the following rows, but make sure to mark the first st of each row.

Row 2: 2 sc in each sc around (12 sts).

Row 3: *2 sc in first st, sc in next st.* Repeat between ** (18 sts).

Row 4: *2 sc in first st, sc in next 2 sts.* Repeat between ** (24 sts).

Row 5: *2 sc in first st, sc in next 3 sts.* Repeat between ** (30 sts).

Continue inc 6 sts in each row until total is 80 sts. Base is approximately 6 inches (15 cm) in diameter.

Body

Work one row sc in back of st. Mark beg of each rnd. Work 1 sc in each sc until piece measures 9 inches (23 cm) above base. Sl st the last st worked to the first st of the last round.

Divide for straps. Sl st across 12 sts. Sc over next 28 sts. Ch 1, turn. Working back and forth over 28 sts, dec 1 st ea end every other row until 8 sts remain. Work on these 8 sts until strap is approximately 14 inches (36 cm) long. Join yarn to the 28 sts at opposite end of bag and repeat for other strap.

Finishing

Sew the two sides of the strap together.

To reinforce behind the snap sections, crochet two squares. With size F hook, ch 5 sts. Sc in second chain from hook and each ch st across. Ch 1, turn (4 sts). Sc in each sc across. Ch 1, turn. Repeat until piece is 1 inch (2.5 cm) long. Install one half of the magnetic snap in the piece by inserting the prongs through the square. With the raffia yarn, sew it to the center of the bag upper edge on the inside. Line up the second snap piece opposite it.

Pin your chosen ornament in place, or stitch it to the bag with the raffia yarn.

CONVERTIBLE BAG

This is a hardworking, thoroughly practical bag, yet it couldn't be easier to make. The upper half folds over to present a neat appearance, or unfolds to work as a spacious tote for shopping or travel. It's practical in other ways, too: it's made of durable cotton canvas to withstand years of laundering and rough handling. Its casual nature is enhanced by the way it is constructed. The carrier and strap have raw edges that are encouraged to ravel when the bag is washed and dried.

The bag itself can be assembled in less than an hour. You might be tempted, though, to spend a full day decorating it. We've added bold geometric appliqué, the pieces outlined with machine blanket stitch. Add your own favorite form of embellishment—with this design, almost anything goes!

The finished bag measures 14 by 21-1/2 inches (35 by 53 cm). The strap is 44 inches (112 cm) long. It can be made any size you wish, just remember to adjust the strap length by the same amount that you change the bag width.

Designer: LORI KERR

MATERIALS

Fabric for the bag and strap, 1 yard (1 m)

Assorted fabric pieces for appliqué

Paper-backed fusible web for appliqué

Decorative thread, if desired, for appliqué and topstitching

INSTRUCTIONS

Preshrink the bag fabric by machine washing and drying it.

Cutting

1. Cut two pieces for the bag front and back, 15 by 22 inches (38 by 54.5 cm). Round off the lower corners, if desired.

2. Cut the strap on the fabric crossgrain, 45 by 4 inches (115 by 10 cm).

3. Cut the carrier on the crossgrain, 14 by 4 inches (35 by 10 cm).

Appliqué

Plan a design that will "read" equally well right side up or upside down.

1. Fuse web to the fabric pieces to be used, following the manufacturer's instructions.

2. Draw the designs on the paper backing and cut out the shapes.

3. Bond the pieces to the upper half of one bag section, keeping clear of the horizontal center of the piece where the carrier will be placed.

4. Stitch the pieces in place with decorative thread and a machine embroidery stitch, or as you choose.

Construction

1. Fold the strap lengthwise, right side out, in thirds, overlapping the raw edges so that the uppermost edge is just short of the fold. Stitch through all thicknesses approximately 1/4 inch (.7 cm) from the raw edge. For security as well as decoration, use a zigzag stitch or open embroidery stitch.

2. Join the ends of the strap by overlapping by approximately 1/2 inch (1.5 cm) and stitching securely.

3. Position part of the strap across the center of the bag section with the appliqué. Place the strap seam so it will be covered by the carrier.

4. Pin the carrier over the strap, centering it between side seam allowances. Stitch the carrier to the bag across both long edges, using the same decorative stitch as for the strap and stitching approximately 1/4 inch (.7 cm) from the edges. Reinforce the ends of the stitching lines with several satin stitches.

5. Fold the bag in half, appliqué toward the front, and arrange the strap so that it is toward the front of the carrier. Stitch through the carrier across the bag slightly behind the strap to help keep the strap in place.

6. At the center of the carrier, stitch through carrier, strap, and bag with satin stitch or several decorative stitches to keep the strap in place.

7. Place the bag sections with right sides together and stitch the sides and bottom, keeping the strap free. Serge or overcast the seam, or use a French seam.

8. Stitch around the top (that same decorative stitch once more) about 1/4 inch (.7 cm) from the raw edge to keep the raveling in check.

9. Pull a few threads from the raw edges, then throw the bag into the washer and dryer to encourage some raveling.

CHAPTER 3

CLASSICS REVISITED

Certain handbag designs are timeless. While hemlines go up or down and waistlines disappear then reappear, there are traditional handbag styles that remain steadfastly with us regardless of the designers' decrees. They suit us. They perform well at their task of keeping together all the paraphernalia we must have close at hand.

The bags shown in this chapter represent several enduring designs. The interpretations, however, are altogether new. Even with a classic there is plenty of room for inventiveness!

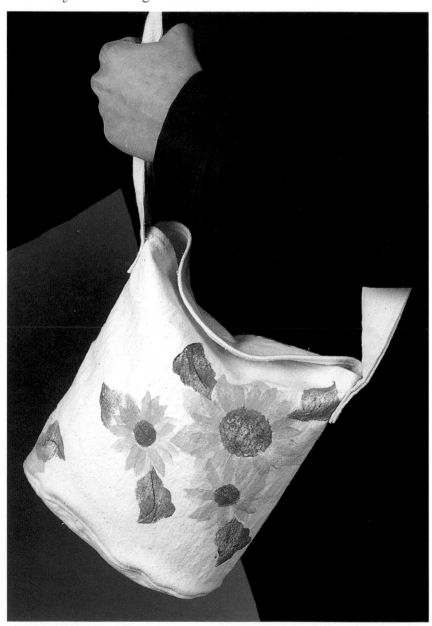

A PERFECT PURSE

Each of us has one: a handbag that is absolutely perfect in every way—or nearly so. Unfortunately, the bag has never been made that will last forever. Why not remake it? This time, improve upon the original with just a few small changes.

This designer's almost-perfect purse drew only two complaints. The lining, naturally, wore out before the outer bag. And it needed just a little more room inside. This time, the outer bag is rich brown pigsuede that presents a conservative face and blends with everything in the wardrobe. The interior is designed with colors to cheer the wearer. The lining and interior pockets are hard-wearing Cordura, trimmed in contrasting lambsuede.

Inside are plenty of pockets. A central section has a zippered pocket for cash, with an open pocket on either side. On one side of the lining is a wide flat pocket. On the other are two deep, pleated pockets for glasses, lined with suede to protect those expensive lenses.

A clever strap attachment prevents the bag tipping its contents onto the floor as you hunt for a credit card. Best of all, a sturdy two-way zipper enables you to open the bag partially or fully, and from the center or from either end.

Designer: DEE DEE TRIPLETT

The finished bag is 8-1/2 inches (21.5 cm) wide, 6 inches (15 cm) high, and 2-1/2 inches (6.5 cm) deep.

MATERIALS AND TOOLS

Use leather or other material that won't ravel, or adjust quantities and measurements to allow for hems.

Pigsuede pieces for the outer bag: for the sides, 10 by 15 inches (25.5 by 38 cm); for the zipper strip and bottom, 4 by 18 inches (10 by 45.5 cm); for the strap, 2 by 40 inches (5 by 102 cm)

Cordura, for the lining: 5/8 yard (.6 m)

Lambsuede: for interior trim and pocket lining, 6 by 12 inches (15 by 30.5 cm); for interior side gussets, 8 by 9 inches (20 by 23 cm)

Parka zipper, 20 inches (51 cm) or longer. This sturdy zipper has teeth rather than coils, and has two pull tabs.

Standard zipper, 7 inches (17.5 cm)

2 eyelets, 1/2 inch (1.3 cm) diameter

2 key rings, 5/8 inch (1.5 cm) diameter

Rawhide, wood, or rubber mallet for pressing leather

Optional, but helpful:

Rotary cutter and mat

Size 90/14 stretch needle, coated, to sew the Cordura

Teflon or roller foot for sewing the leather

Silicon lubricant

INSTRUCTIONS

Please read the tips on working with leather, page 19. Seam allowances are 1/2 inch (1.3 cm) except as noted. Enlarge the pattern pieces and cut them from paper.

Zipper and bottom

1. Destroy the parka zipper and reassemble it. Cut the stops off both ends. Remove one zipper pull. Open the zipper at other end about 3 inches (7.5 cm). Replace the other zipper pull so the two are head to head and will open the zipper in both directions from the center. Note that zipper teeth are not level or even on the end. Feed the zipper tooth on the longer side of the zipper tape into the zipper pull first, then the tooth on the remaining side. An extra set of hands is very helpful. If this terrifies you, you can use a regular zipper—the purse will just be a bit more difficult to get into.

2. Make the zipper strip and bottom of the purse. Cut two strips each of suede and lining, 2 by 18 inches (5 by 45.5 cm). Cut one strip of suede and of lining 3-1/2 by 11-1/2 inches (9 by 29 cm) for the bottom.

3. Do not cut the zipper to length yet. Move the zipper pulls beyond the 18-inch (45.5-cm) area that will be sewn so they are out of the way. Matching long edges, layer one piece of zipper strip lining right side up, then

THE MODEL FOR THE PERFECT PURSE SERVED LONG AND WELL.

the zipper right side up, then one suede strip right side down as shown. Sew one side of the zipper. Repeat for the other side of the zipper.

4. Fold the lining and suede away from the zipper on each side and topstitch about 3/8 inch (1 cm) from the zipper teeth. (The teeth will show.) Trim the whole zipper strip to 3-1/2 inches (9 cm) wide.

5. Move the zipper pulls to the center. Overcast both ends of the zipper securely then cut off the excess.

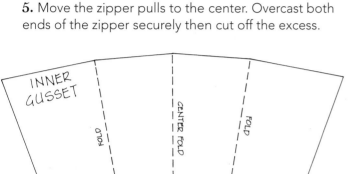

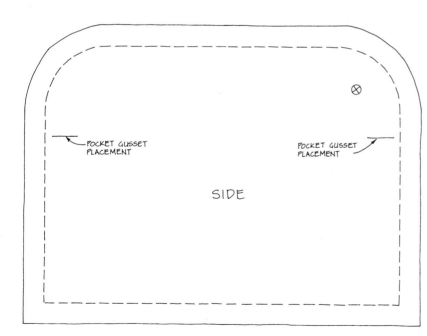

PATTERN, INNER GUSSET (ABOVE) AND THE PERFECT PURSE SIDES.
ENLARGE 222%.

6. Join the zipper strip to the purse bottom at the narrow ends. Layer the pieces: the bottom lining, right side up, the zipper strip right side up, and the suede right side down. Stitch from the zipper teeth to one edge, then from the teeth to the other edge. This will form a circle.

Sides and lining

1. From the pattern, cut two side pieces of suede and two of lining.

2. Cut the glasses pocket piece and its lining. For the pocket, cut bag lining fabric 10 by 5-3/8 inches (25.5 by 13.5 cm). For the pocket lining, cut lambsuede 10 by 5-7/8 inches (25.5 by 15 cm).

3. With right sides together and 1/4 inch (.5 cm) seam allowance, sew one long side of the suede to the lining. Trim, and fold the suede to the wrong side of the lining, allowing suede to show about 1/4 inch (.5 cm). Stitch in the ditch to secure. Fold under the remaining three edges of the lined pocket 1/4 inch (.5 cm).

4. Chalk mark the center of one purse lining section and the center of the glasses pocket. Measure 2-3/4 inches (7 cm) to each side of center on the purse lining and draw a vertical line.

5. Position the pocket on the lining, aligning center lines and with the top of the pocket 3/4 inch (2 cm) below the top of the lining. Sew the pocket to the purse lining down the center of the pocket. Sew left edge down the line marked to left of center, and the right edge on the line to right. Fold pleats for ease along the bottom of each pocket and sew across bottom of pocket.

6. For the pocket on the other lining section, cut one piece of purse lining 4 by 7 inches (10 by 18 cm), and a strip of lambsuede 1 by 7 inches (2.5 by 18 cm).

7. Sew the trim across a long edge of the pocket, right sides together. Turn right sides out, and stitch in the ditch to secure. Turn under the remaining three sides 1/4 inch (.5 cm) and sew to the center of the purse lining piece.

Center pockets

1. Make the zippered pocket and its two side pockets. Cut one piece of bag lining 7 inches (17.5 cm) square. Cut two pieces 9 by 13 inches (22.5 cm by 33 cm).

2. Sew the wrong side of the zipper to two opposite right sides of the square fabric, forming a tube. (The right side of lining fabric will end up inside the zippered pocket.)

3. To add the adjacent pockets and to complete the zippered pocket, fold and mark these pieces as shown.

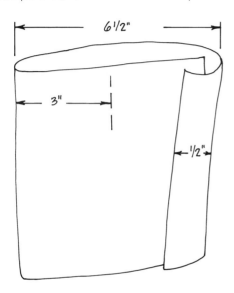

4. Sew the folded piece along the right side of the zipper tape as shown, tucking under the tape ends and stitching them into the seam. Repeat for the other side.

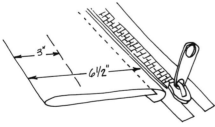

5. Sew the two open ends of the zippered pocket, using a narrow seam allowance and keeping the adjacent pockets free.

Assembling the parts

1. Sew the purse sides to the zipper/bottom strip. Open the zipper. Begin at the center of the bottom and sew each way, clipping corners as needed. The seams connecting zipper strip and bottom should end up 1-1/2 inches (4 cm) up from the bottom of the purse sides. Trim and serge or overcast the seam allowances.

2. For the interior gussets, cut two pieces of lambsuede trim from the pattern. Chalk mark the three foldlines as shown on pattern.

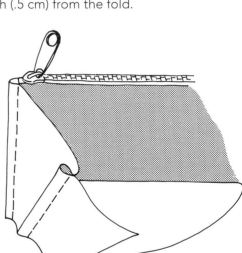

3. Fold one gusset on the center fold-line and wrap that fold around an end of the center zippered pocket, keeping the side pockets free. Stitch through all layers approximately 1/4 inch (.5 cm) from the fold.

4. Now fold up one of the remaining 3-inch (7.5 cm) pockets and wrap and stitch it into the adjacent gusset fold as illustrated. Repeat for the other side pocket, and at the other end.

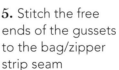

5. Stitch the free ends of the gussets to the bag/zipper strip seam allowances, placing the lower ends of the gussets approximately 1/2 inch (1.5 cm) above the bottom of the bag.

Strap and finishing

1. Fold the strap in half lengthwise, right side out. Tap with the mallet to press. Fold the edge in to the center crease; press. Stitch along both edges.

2. Attach the eyelets. Make a small hole in one upper corner of one side of the purse. Repeat on opposite corner of other side. Attach an eyelet in each hole.

3. Thread one end of the strap through each eyelet. Fold each end over one of the miniature key rings and stitch to hold. The rings will prevent the strap from pulling out of the eyelets, and will provide a spot for attaching keys.

ORIGAMI ENVELOPE

Sometimes the fabric itself suggests a design. This one began with a remnant of soft cotton upholstery fabric, a woven plaid with wonderful texture and good neutral colors. The designer experimented with the cloth, folding it this way and that, until the finished bag took shape. The folds follow the lines of the plaid, with the colors arranged in a pleasing way.

The strap is stuffed tubing, coiled into a complementary circular shape where it is attached to the bag. An additional length of tubing is incorporated into the bow on the flap. For the cleverest of closures, two small magnets are covered with fabric and stitched to the bag front and underside of the flap.

The bag is self lined. The fabric piece was doubled to determine placement of the folds of the bag. Before the folds were stitched, pieces of thin batting were cut to shape and placed between the lining and outer fabric layers. Machine stitching holds the outer folds in place. Inside, the layers were hand sewn.

A zipper is not essential, but one is included in this bag. It was installed after the bag was sewn together. One side of the zipper was stitched by machine, right side up, under the front of the bag, the bag edge along the stitching line of the zipper tape. The remaining side of the zipper was stitched by hand to the foldline along the underside of the flap.

Plaids, stripes, checks, and geometric prints all would work well for this design. Experiment with the fabric itself and chalk mark the foldlines to determine the cutting lines for the batting. Or use a large piece of paper to try out several different folding schemes. As many times as you may try this design, no two bags could ever be exactly the same.

Designer: NELL PAULK

FREE-SPIRITED LEATHER HANDBAG

Wonderful effects can be created when you play with the irregular shapes and lines inherent in a piece of leather. This bag design is altogether traditional, but the interpretation is unique and charming.

The front of the bag is in two pieces, one overlapping the other, glued along the vertical edge and stitched into the lining and bottom seams. Pleats at each side shape the top. The pleats are stitched with leather cord and secured with handmade pewter beads. Across the flap, decorative stitching is worked by hand with the cord. A pewter button is added for accent.

The cowhide chosen for the bag is slightly heavier than garment-weight leather, but works in this case because no seam includes more than two layers. The bag is 14 inches (35.5 cm) wide at the bottom and 9 inches (23 cm) high.

Designer: LOIS ERICSON

MATERIALS AND TOOLS

Leather, medium weight, quantity according to cutting measurements below.

Lining fabric, 3/8 yard (.35 m)

Beads, buttons or other interesting ornaments

Waxed leather cord, approximately 3 yards (2.75 m). As an alternative, use another strong, decorative cord.

Contact cement

Rubber, rawhide, or wood mallet for pressing

Glover's needle, large enough to accommodate the leather cord

Binder clamps

INSTRUCTIONS

Please read the detailed information on sewing with leather, page 19.

Designing

It would be difficult to duplicate this bag exactly. Instead, let it serve as inspiration for your own experimentation. Start with a piece of leather that has interesting irregular edges and see what it might become. Play with the shapes, arrange the edges in different ways, look for other intriguing materials to incorporate in the design.

Cutting

1. For the bag front and back, cut two leather pieces approximately 15 inches (38 cm) wide and 9-1/2 inches (24 cm) long. If you wish, piece scraps to these dimensions, stitching them together or overlapping the edges and gluing with the contact cement.

2. For the straps, cut two pieces 1 inch (2.5 cm) wide and 29 inches (73 cm) long, or as needed.

3. For the flap, use an irregularly shaped scrap, or cut a piece approximately 8 inches (20 cm) wide and 12 inches (30.5 cm) long.

4. Cut two lining pieces 15 inches (38 cm) wide and 10 inches (25.5 cm) long.

5. If desired, cut a pocket for the lining.

Construction

1. Piece leather for the bag front and back according to your design. For the model, two overlapped pieces make up the bag front. They are glued almost to the edge of the overlapping piece, then stitched as one in the bottom and lining seams. An additional smaller scrap decorates the front, stitched into the upper seam and left free at the lower edge.

2. With right sides together and 1/2 inch (1.5 cm) seam allowance, stitch the front to the back. Round the lower corners or sew them on the diagonal for shaping and easier turning. Tap seams open with the mallet to press.

3. Make and attach the lining pocket. Stitch the lining front and back, shaping the corners as for the bag. Trim, turn, and press.

4. Fold the lining upper edge 1 inch (2.5 cm) to the wrong side; press.

5. Place the lining in the bag and stitch around the upper edge.

6. Make the straps. Fold each piece lengthwise, right side out. Stitch fairly close to the raw edges, beginning and ending the stitching approximately 2 inches (5 cm) from the ends.

7. Fold a 1-inch (2.5 cm) pleat on each side of each side seam. Clamp in place. Position an end of one strap on the bag front at the pleated area, and an end of the other strap at the back. With the glover's needle and cord, take a hand stitch through all the thicknesses, knotting securely at both ends. Add beads at the cord ends if desired. Make another stitch through the

layers in the same way. Attach the other strap ends at the other side of the bag.

8. Plan the flap so that it will extend well over the top opening of the bag. Decorate it according to your plan. On the back, glue it in place, or stitch it, to within approximately 1 inch (2.5 cm) of the bag opening.

PEARL-HANDLED BAG

Shimmery hand-dyed rayon cord in soft, variegated hues makes a very feminine little bag. It is crocheted onto purchased handles in a complementary pearlized shade, with a matching button closure. The shoulder strap can be looped through the handles for wearing, or can be knotted and left to dangle.

The finished bag is approximately 8 inches (20 cm) wide and 7 inches (17 cm) high, handles included.

Designer: JUDI ALWEIL

Materials and Tools

- Handles, 4 inches (10 cm), with pre-drilled holes
- Shank button to match, 5/8 inch (1.5 cm) diameter
- Rayon cord or cordé yarn, 144 yards (132 m)
- Crochet hook, U.S. size F
- Yarn needle
- Fabric adhesive
- Lining fabric (optional): 1/4 yard (.25m)

Instructions

Crochet abbreviations are explained on page 59.

Front and back

Make two pieces.

With hook, attach yarn to 1st hole in handle. Sc in each hole (10 sts). Ch 1; turn.

Row 1: Inc in each st by making 2 sts in each st (20 sts). Ch 1; turn.

Row 2: Inc in every 5th st (24 sts). Ch 1; turn.

Row 3: Inc in every 6th st (28 sts). Ch 1; turn.

Row 4 and remaining rows: Work even until piece measures 4-3/4 inches (12 cm). Bind off.

Gusset

Chain 4; turn.

Row 1: Sc in 2nd ch from hook and each ch across (3 sts). Ch 1; turn.

Row 2: Sc in each chain across. Ch 1; turn.

Repeat row 2 until gusset measures approximately 16 inches (40.5 cm). Do not break yarn.

Assembly

Hold the bag front or back and the gusset with right sides together. Start at the beginning end of the gusset and whipstitch the two together, using a strand of the yarn. Adjust the gusset length. Add the other bag section. Weave in the yarn ends.

Button and loop

At the inside center on one side of the bag, attach yarn just below the handle and work a chain approximately 3 inches (7.5 cm) long. Fold in half and sl st at the beginning point. Sew the button on the opposite side, on the outside of the bag.

Shoulder strap

Attach yarn at the top of a side gusset. Chain 45 inches (114 cm). Attach with slip stitch to the other side gusset. Slip stitch in each ch back to the beginning; fasten off.

Optional lining

Lining will help the bag retain its shape, and allows you to add a small pocket or two if you wish.

1. Fold the lining fabric piece in half, lengthwise. Place the finished bag on the fabric with one side along the fold, and smooth it flat. Chalk mark the outline of the bag. At the top, mark a line even with the tops of the gussets, then add 1 inch (2.5 cm) for a hem.

2. Straighten the lines and cut. There is no need to add seam allowance—the difference in the inner and outer dimensions of the bag will allow for the seams.

3. Add a pocket if you wish (see page 5 for some suggestions).

4. Stitch across the bottom and up the side, using approximately 1/4 inch (.5 cm) seam allowance.

5. Fit the lining into the bag; there should be a little ease. Fold under the upper edge to approximately 3/8 inch (1 cm) below the top of the bag.

6. Whipstitch the lining in place.

Designer: LORI KERR

A TRIO OF BUCKET BAGS

Bucket bags have been in and out of the fashion scene for decades. Whatever their current status, the simple styling can't be topped for convenience: flip it open, and the contents are within easy reach.

The basic bag is easy and quick to make, and it can be varied in dozens of ways. Add a lining (and a pocket or two) or leave it unlined; make the strap long or short, narrow or wide. Add outside pockets, add an exotic closure, and add whatever kind of embellishment that occurs to you. It's a very adaptable sort of design!

THE BASIC BUCKET

Finished bag is 10 inches (25.5 cm) wide and 8-1/2 inches (21.5 cm) high. The strap is 1 1/2 inches (4 cm) wide, 38 inches (96 cm) in length.

MATERIALS

Fabric: 1/2 yard (.5 m)

Optional lining: 1/2 yard (.5 m)

INSTRUCTIONS: An Unlined Bag

Seam allowance is 3/8 inch (1 cm).

1. Enlarge the pattern and cut from paper.

2. Cut two sides and one bottom by the pattern. Cut the strap on the lengthwise grain of the fabric (piece if necessary) 2-1/4 inches (6 cm) wide and 40 inches (102 cm) long.

3. Hem the upper (curved) edges of each side piece with a 5/8-inch (1.5-cm) double hem.

4. Stitch the side seams. Use French seams, or stitch a standard seam then overcast the seam allowances together and stitch them down.

5. Fold the bottom section in half lengthwise and mark the crease point at each end. Sew to the bag with right sides together, matching the marks to the side seams.

6. Fold the strap in half lengthwise, wrong side out. Stitch the long edge. Trim; turn. Turn under the seam allowances at the ends. Topstitch all edges. As an alternative, fold in the seam allowances, press, and edgestitch closed. Edgestitch the opposite long edge and the ends.

7. Either on the inside or outside of the bag, position the strap ends over the side seamlines approximately 1 inch (2.5 cm) below the bag edge. Stitch securely in place, around the edges and with an X.

A Lined Bag

A pocket can be added to one or both sides of the lining. Suggestions are on page 5.

1. Enlarge the pattern and cut from paper.

2. From outer fabric, cut two sides and one bottom by the pattern. Cut the strap on the lengthwise grain of the fabric (piece if necessary) 2-1/4 inches (6 cm) wide and 40 inches (102 cm) long. Cut two sides and one bottom from lining.

3. Stitch the outer bag side seams with right sides together.

4. Fold the bottom section in half lengthwise and mark the crease point at each end. Sew to the bag with right sides together, matching the marks to the side seams.

5. Stitch the lining side seams, leaving a generous opening on one side for turning.

6. Sew the lining bottom in place.

7. With right sides together, place the bag inside the lining. Stitch around the upper edge. Trim, turn, and topstitch. Whipstitch the opening in the lining.

8. Fold the strap in half lengthwise, wrong side out. Stitch the long edge. Trim; turn. Turn under the seam allowances at the ends. Topstitch all edges. As an alternative, fold in the seam allowances, press, and edgestitch closed. Edgestitch the opposite long edge and the ends.

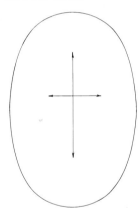

9. Either on the inside or outside of the bag, position the strap ends over the side seamlines approximately 1 inch (2.5 cm) below the bag edge. Stitch each end securely in place, around the edges and with an X.

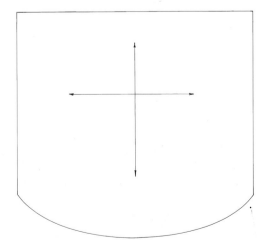

PATTERN, BUCKET BAG BOTTOM (ABOVE) AND SIDES. ENLARGE 500%.

Painted Bucket Bag

No matter that you don't have a shred of artistic ability—you can still personalize your very basic bag with a colorful design. Precut sponges, available in craft supply stores, provide the shapes. Fabric paints do the rest!

This bag is sturdy cotton duck fabric, prewashed so the paint would penetrate the surface. The design was applied to the individual pieces before the bag was assembled. The paints used here called for heat-setting. Check directions on the containers to be sure the paint is compatible with the fabric you plan to use.

Leather Bucket Bag

Because leather doesn't ravel, construction time is shortened by several steps. Garment-weight leather isn't at all difficult to sew. Follow the guidelines on page 19 for great results.

Our leather bag was made of leather scraps in assorted colors and thicknesses. The strap is fairly heavy, so only a single thickness was used, cut to

Designer: **Lor Kerr**

the finished width measurement. If piecing is necessary to obtain the length, ends can be overlapped by approximately 1 inch (2.5 cm) and stitched with a square and an X. For thinner leather, cut the strap twice the desired finished width, fold it right side out, then topstitch both long edges.

The sides and bottom are sewn with right sides together as usual. The seam allowances were graded, then pressed to one side and stitched in place.

On this bag, the flap edges were left unhemmed. With lighter weight leather, stitch a single hem, then trim to the stitching. The designer suggests not using the lightest color for the bottom of the bag—unless you plan never to set it down!

As a variation on this theme, smaller leather scraps could be pieced to make up the sides and bottom of the bag. A geometric quilt-block look would be interesting; stripes or design shapes of lightweight leathers might be combined to give the look of applique.

Designer: **Lor Kerr**

PATCHWORK BUCKET BAG (shown on page 52)

An altogether different effect is created when the basic bag is assembled of bright cotton prints, layered and stitched with metallic and rayon threads. An inner layer of batting gives dimension to the quilting and adds support to the lightweight fabrics. Layered squares, stitched in the technique made popular by Bird Ross, cover the seamlines.

The construction is similar to that of the basic bag described previously, but with a few differences.

MATERIALS AND TOOLS

Fabrics: Use complementary lightweight cottons for the bag, lining, and strap. For the accent pieces, you will need approximately 1/4 yard (.25 m) additional.

Garment-weight batting, 1/2 yard (.5 m)

Assorted decorative threads: metallic, variegated, or rayon in several colors

Optional (see step 4)

Lightweight fusible interfacing: 1/4 yard (.25 m)

Wavy blade for rotary cutter

INSTRUCTIONS

1. Cut fabric for the strap twice the desired finished width (seam allowances aren't needed). Cut batting to the finished width measurement.

2. Cut lining for the bottom and two sides by the pattern. Trim off hem allowance at the flap edges.

3. Cut outer fabric and batting according to the pattern, but trim away seam and hem allowances.

4. For the accent pieces, cut approximately 40 squares, 2 to 2-1/2 inches (5 to 6.5 cm). On the bag shown, the accent fabric was first fused to lightweight interfacing and the squares cut using a wavy blade in the rotary cutter. Without the interfacing, the raw edges of the small pieces can be encouraged to ravel, adding texture to the bag.

5. Assemble the lining according to the instructions for the basic bag. Press the seams open.

6. Layer the batting and the outer bag sections with the outer fabric right side up. Position each pair on the wrong side of the appropriate lining section so the batting is sandwiched between the fabrics.

Pin at intervals and machine quilt lightly to hold the layers together.

7. Now the fun begins. Cover the seamlines at the sides and around the bottom with the accent squares. Place one square diagonally over the seamline. With decorative thread, stitch it heavily to the bag, stitching back and forth over the edges. Add the next square, overlapping the first, and stitch it. Continue along the seam this way. Along each flap edge, fold the squares diagonally over the edge, overlapping the corners, and stitch in the same way.

8. Fold the strap fabric right side out around the batting. Baste the long edges together. Fold accent squares diagonally around the strap raw edge as for the bag flap, and stitch them in place. Attach the strap at the sides seams, covering the ends with accent squares.

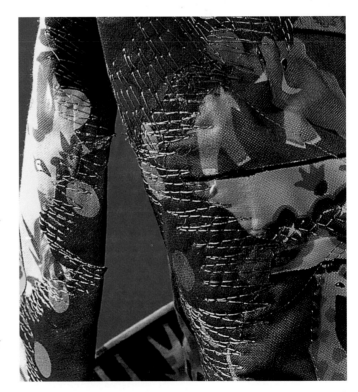

QUILTED PURSE

A fitting companion for business suits and dresses, this impeccably tailored purse always looks stylish. The fabric is rayon and wool blend gabardine, durable and quite dressy. It is quilted to light-weight batting on the front, back, and sides. For the strap, a stuffed fabric tube is laced through a gold tone chain and fastened to the bag with small swivel hooks. A gold pin adorns the flap to cover the snap. The finished bag is 10 (25.5 cm) inches wide across the top and 9-1/2 inches (24 cm) high.

MATERIALS

Fabric for outer bag: 3/8 yard (.35 m)

Lining fabric: 3/8 yard (.35 m)

Muslin, 3/8 yard (.35 m)

Garment weight batting: 3/8 yard (.35 m)

Fusible interfacing: 3/4 yard (.7 m)

Cotton cording: 2-1/2 yards (2.3 m), 1/4 inch (.7 cm) diameter

Plastic mesh: 10-5/8 by 13-5/8 inches (27 by 34.5 cm)

Large snap

Decorative chain with 3/8 to 5/8 inch (1 to 1.5 cm) links, approximately 54 inches (137 cm) long

2 metal D-rings, 3/4 inch (2 cm) diameter

2 small metal swivel hooks

2 metal end caps with end loops

2 metal jump rings to join end cap loops to swivel snap (can be made from 16-gauge wire)

Decorative pin for flap

Jewelry pliers or needlenose pliers

Cyanoacrylate glue

Designer: DAWN ANDERSON

INSTRUCTIONS

Enlarge the pattern for the purse flap and cut it from paper. Make a paper pattern for the front and back. Draw a rectangle 9 inches (23 cm) wide and 10 inches (25.5 cm) high. On the bottom line, mark a point 1-1/2 inches (4 cm) in from each side. Connect these points with the upper corners to make the piece a trapezoid shape. Mark the bottom center. Mark a point on each side 4-1/4 inches (11 cm) up from the bottom. Round the lower corners (use a large thread spool or something similar). Add 1/2 inch (1.5 cm) seam allowance on all sides.

Cutting

1. From bag fabric, cut two pieces for the bag front and back, cutting approximately 1/2 inch (1.5 cm) larger than the pattern all around to allow for quilting. Transfer the marked points.

2. Cut two flap pieces, approximately 1/2 inch (1.5 cm) larger all around than the pattern. Mark the center of the lower seamline (seam allowance of 1/2 inch (1.5 cm) is included on the pattern).

3. For the sides, cut two rectangles 3 inches (7.5 cm) by 10-1/8 inches (25.5 cm).

4. For the bottom, cut one rectangle 3 inches by 8-1/8 inches.

5. For the strap, cut a strip on the lengthwise fabric grain 2 inches by 42 inches (5 cm by 107 cm).

6. Cut two squares, 2-1/2 inches (6.5 cm), for D-ring loops.

7. Cut two pieces each of muslin and batting for the front and back, using the fabric piece as a guide.

8. Cut one piece of muslin and one of batting for the flap, using the fabric piece as a guide.

9. The lining and those bag pieces that are not quilted will be interfaced. Cut two pieces of fusible interfacing for the sides, using the measurements above. Cut one piece for the bottom. Cut front and back interfacing by the pattern for just the lining pieces. For the flap facing, cut one piece by the flap pattern and also cut a 2-inch (5-cm) strip to fit between the foldlines. For the lining side/bottom interfacing, cut according to the measurements in step 9. Cut two 2-1/2 inch (4 cm) squares for the D-rings.

10. From batting and from muslin, cut two pieces each from the front/back pattern. Cut one piece of each from the flap pattern. Cut one piece of each 3 inches (7.5 cm) by 27-1/4 inches (69 cm) for the sides and bottom.

11. From plastic mesh, cut two pieces 1-7/8 by 8-3/8 inches (4.75 by 21 cm) for the sides. Cut one piece 1-7/8 by 6-1/8 inches (4.75 by 15.5 cm) for the bottom.

12. From lining fabric, cut front and back by the pattern. Cut a side/bottom piece using the measurements in step 9. Cut a pocket 8 inches (20 cm) square.

Quilting

1. Quilt the front and back pieces. Layer muslin, batting, and fabric right side up. Pin at intervals with safety pins. For the quilting pattern shown on the model, begin stitching at the marked center on the lower seamline and stitch to the marked point at one side seamline. Stitch parallel lines at 1-3/4-inch (4.5-cm)

intervals, stitching parallel lines in the same direction. Trim the quilted pieces to the pattern.

2. Quilt one (upper) flap piece the same way. Trim the piece 1/8 inch (.3 cm) larger than the pattern at the sides and front so it will roll toward the facing.

Assembling the bag

Seam allowances are 1/2 inch (1.5 cm) except as indicated otherwise.

1. Apply interfacing to the wrong sides of the purse side and bottom pieces following the manufacturer's directions. Stitch one end of each side section to the bottom with right sides together. Press seam allowances open. On the right side, edgestitch both sides of each seam.

2. Place the batting, then muslin, on the wrong side of the side/bottom piece. Baste in the seam allowance.

3. Pin the side/bottom strip to the purse back with right sides together. Ease in fullness around curves, clipping as necessary. Stitch. Press seam allowances open. Trim; notch around curves. Repeat for front.

4. Center and pin a plastic mesh piece to the purse bottom under the seam allowances. Handstitch in place to seam allowances on the sides and to muslin on the ends. Apply mesh to the sides in the same way, with the upper ends of the pieces 1/8 inch (.3 cm) below the seamline.

5. Apply interfacing to the flap facing. Apply the additional strip between the foldlines.

6. Stitch the flap and facing with right sides together, stretching the facing slightly to fit and leaving an opening on the straight side. Grade seam allowances; notch curves. Turn right side out; press. Slipstitch the opening.

7. Shape folds in the flap by steam pressing over the edge of the ironing board. Allow the piece to cool.

8. Position the flap over top of the purse, aligning quilted stitching lines at front. Pin the flap to the purse back, the flap straight edge approximately 1-1/4 inches (3 cm) below the purse edge. Edgestitch to the purse along the flap straight edge, and stitch again 1/4 inch (.5 cm) away.

9. Fuse interfacing to the wrong sides of each D-ring loop piece. Fold the piece in half, right sides together, and stitch. Press seam allowances open; trim. Turn right side out. Press again, centering the seam allowance.

10. Slip a D-ring onto each piece and fold the strip in half. Center a loop on the right side of each bag side, raw edges aligned. Baste.

Lining

1. Apply interfacing to the wrong sides of lining pieces.

2. Make the pocket. Hem one long edge with a wide double hem. On the remaining edges, press the seam allowances to the wrong side. Position on one (back) lining section approximately 1-1/2 inches (4 cm) below the upper edge. Edgestitch in place. Trim seam allowances, then stitch again 1/4 inch (.5 cm) from first stitching.

3. Because of the thickness of the quilted outer bag, it may be necessary to use larger seam allowances for the lining so it is not too full. Pin-fit or baste the side/front and side/back seams before stitching.

4. Pin the lining side/bottom piece to the lining back, right sides together, easing in fullness around corners. Stitch; press seam allowances toward the bottom and side. Repeat for the front, leaving a long opening on one side for turning.

5. With right sides together, insert the purse into the lining. Stitch around the upper edge. Trim seam allowances. Turn right side out through the opening. Understitch the lining to the seam allowance around the upper edge of purse. Slipstitch the opening.

6. To attach the lining, stitch in the ditch in the four side seams, beginning 1/8 inch (.5 cm) from the upper edge and ending about 1 inch (2.5 cm) below.

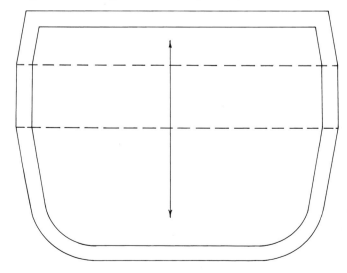

PATTERN, QUILTED PURSE FLAP. ENLARGE 334%.

7. Sew a snap section (cover it with lining fabric for a couturier touch) at the center front of the bag, approximately 1-3/4 inches (4.5 cm) below the edge. Sew the other piece in the corresponding spot on the underside of the flap, allowing a little ease so that when the bag is filled it will still close neatly.

Strap

1. Cut cording twice the length of the strap fabric. Fold the fabric, wrong side out, around the cord. Using a zipper foot, stitch along the cord, but not too close to it. Some ease will be needed for turning. At one end, stitch securely across the fabric and through the cord. On the long edge, trim seam allowances close to stitching. Turn the tube right side out by sliding the strip over the cord. Trim the cord at the ends.

2. Beginning at the center of the chain, weave the cord through it toward both ends. Remove extra chain links at the ends. Apply epoxy to the ends of the cord and inside the end caps. Press the caps over the cord ends and allow to dry.

3. Secure the chain to each swivel snap with an extra chain link. Connect the end cap loop to the swivel snap with a jump ring.

CHAPTER 4

BAGS TO KNIT AND CROCHET

Crocheted and knitted patterns produce wonderful surface textures that look especially good in handbags. The resulting fabric, particularly when created

of sturdier yarns, wears well and has just enough give to accommodate the assortment of shapes we often stuff into our bags.

The designs offered in this chapter are all quite simple to work. Most of them are quick to make besides. They are shown in a variety of unusual yarns that contribute to their good looks.

Knitting and Crochet Abbreviations

beg	beginning	**rnd**	round
dec	decrease	**rs**	right side
inc	increase	**st(s)**	stitch(es)
ndl	needle	**ws**	wrong side

* * or ( ) repeat the steps described between asterisks or parentheses the number of times instructed

Crochet stitches

ch	chain
dc	double crochet
hdc	half double crochet
sc	single crochet
sl	slip
tc	triple (treble) crochet

Knitting stitches

K	knit
P	purl

CHERRY-RED DRAWSTRING BAG

The style is as carefree as the color, guaranteed to add a note of cheer to a conservative outfit or perk up a dreary day. A pretty scalloped pattern edges the top, and the drawstring and shoulder strap are twisted cord.

At 4-1/2 inches (11.5 cm) in diameter and 7 inches (18 cm) deep, it is sized to hold a billfold and a few other necessities. It is quick to crochet in rayon cordé yarn.

Designer: JUDI ALWEIL

MATERIALS AND TOOLS

Rayon cordé, 144 yards (132 m)

Crochet hook, U.S. size F

Optional: fabric for lining, 1/4 yard (.25 m)

INSTRUCTIONS

Crochet abbreviations are explained on page 59.

Pattern stitches:

Single crochet

Double crochet in back loop

Note: Do not join rounds. Mark the beginning of each round with a safety pin.

Base

Ch 4, join with sl st to form ring, ch 1.

Rnd 1: Work 7 sc in ring.

Rnd 2: Work 2 sc into each sc around (14 sc).

Rnd 3: Work *2 sc in 1st sc, 1 sc in next sc* around (21 sc).

Rnd 4: Work *2 sc in 1st sc, 1 in each of next 2 sc* around (28 sc).

Rnd 5: Work *2 sc in 1st sc, 1 in each of next 3* around (35 sc).

Rnd 6: Work *2 sc in 1st sc, 1 in each of next 4* around (42 sc).

Rnd 7: Work *2 sc in 1st sc, 1 in each of next 5* around (49 sc).

Rnd 8: Work 1 round sc even.

The base should measure 4-1/2 inches (11.5 cm) in diameter.

Body

Rnd 9: ch 3; working in bar below back loop, *dc in each of next 3 sts, then dc twice in 4th st* around. Join with sl st to top of ch 3 (61 dc, counting ch 3 as dc).

Rnds 10-18: ch 3, dc in back loop of each dc in row below, end with sl st in top of ch 3.

Scalloped border

Slip st in 1st stitch, skip 1 stitch, 4 sc in next stitch, skip 1 stitch around, 15 times. End with slip stitch in same stitch as beginning slip stitch. Fasten off.

Drawstring

Make two. Cut a 2-yard (1.85-m) length of cordé and make a twisted cord. Fold it in half and loop it over a doorknob or something stationary. Twist the cord in one direction very tightly. Keeping the cord taut, bring the free end to the attached end and allow it to double up on itself. Knot the cut end.

Weave one cord through the stitching, beginning with the second to last round of dc, over 3 dc, then under 3, bringing it out 3 sts before the beginning point. Repeat with the other cord, beginning and ending on the opposite side of the bag, but weaving over and under the same stitches. Knot the ends of each cord together.

Shoulder strap

Cut a 7-yard (6.4-m) length of cordé. Fold it in half, then make twisted cord approximately 53 inches (134 cm) long. Make a knot approximately 3 inches (7.5 cm) from each end, then use the ends to attach the strap to the inside of the bag at the point on each side where the drawstrings meet.

Lining

A lining is not essential, but lining looks tidy and will keep small items from catching in the threads of the bag.

1. Fold the lining fabric piece in half, lengthwise. Place the finished bag on the fabric with one side along the fold, and smooth it flat. Chalk mark the outline of the bag. Mark just below the drawstring channel for the finished upper edge, then add approximately 1 inch (2.5 cm) above that for hem allowance.

2. Straighten the lines and cut. There is no need to add seam allowance—the difference in the inner and outer dimensions of the bag will allow for the seams.

3. Stitch across the bottom and up the side using approximately 1/4 inch (.5 cm) seam allowance. Clean-finish the seams.

4. Fit the lining into the bag; there should be a little ease. Fold under the hem at the upper edge and whip-stitch in place just below the drawstring channel.

Designer: JUDI ALWEIL

CABLE-PATTERNED BAG

The pattern may look complicated—it's knitted side to side—but this bag knits up so quickly that it is an ideal project for occasions when you need to make a special gift in a hurry. The yarn is a lustrous rayon cord that highlights the rich texture of the pattern. The finished bag measures approximately 5-1/2 by 7-1/2 inches (14 by 19 cm).

MATERIALS

Rayon cordé, 144 yards (132 m)

Needles, U.S. size 6, or size to give gauge

Cable needle

Crochet hook, U.S. size G

Lining fabric, 1/4 yard (.25 m)

Magnetic snap

INSTRUCTIONS
Knitting abbreviations are defined on page 59.

Gauge: 4 sts to 1 inch

Seed stitch pattern:

Row 1 (and odd-numbered rows): k1, p1

Row 2 (and even-numbered rows): p1, k1

Front and back
Make two pieces.

On no. 6 ndl, cast on 34 sts

Rows 1, 3, 5: Seed 8 sts, k6, seed 8 sts, k6

Rows 2, 4, 6: Seed 6, p6, Seed 8 sts

Row 7: Seed 8 sts. Twist cable: slip 3 sts to cable ndl and hold in back, k3 sts, k3 from cable ndl. Seed 8 sts, twist cable, seed 6 sts.

Row 8: Same as row 2.

Repeat these 8 rows until piece measures 6 inches (15 cm). Bind off loosely.

Gusset and shoulder strap
A single knitted strip forms the strap and the gusset along the bag sides and bottom. Determine the finished length you will need, allowing for some stretch.

1. Cast on 4 sts. Knit in garter stitch (k all rows) until piece measures 57 inches (144 cm) or desired length. Place the stitches on a holder in case adjustment in length is needed later.

2. Hold the bag back and the strip with right sides together. Thread a yarn needle with a strand of the cord. Beginning at one upper corner of the bag back, on the wrong side, and with the cast on end of the gusset, whipstitch the gusset to the bag, down the side, across the bottom, and up the other side. Whipstitch the front to the gusset in the same way, matching the front and back pattern across the gusset.

3. Attach the end of the strap to the starting end of the gusset. Work 1 row sc across the top of the bag.

Lining
To give the bag more body and keep the inside neat, make a pretty lining. We used cotton/rayon moiré in a matching color. For a sportier effect, try striped or pat-terned cotton. Add a pocket before stitching the lining seam if you wish.

1. Fold the lining fabric piece in half, lengthwise. Position the bag on the fabric with one side along the fabric fold, and smooth the bag flat. Chalk mark the outline of the bag.

2. Straighten the lines, then cut the fabric. The difference between the inner and outer dimensions of the bag make it unnecessary to add seam allowance.

3. Stitch across the bottom and up the side using approximately 1/4 inch (.5 cm) seam allowance. Try the fit, leaving a little ease.

4. Pin the lining in the bag. Mark the position of the snap sections at lining center front and back, approximately 1 inch (2.5 cm) below the upper edges. Place a pin to mark the position on the outside of the bag, too.

5. Fold under the upper edge of the lining to approximately 3/8 inch (1 cm) from the top. Pin the hem. Remove the lining from the bag and press the hem.

6. Press the fold, then whipstitch the lining in place around the bag opening.

The fastener
1. Crochet two reinforcement pieces for the snap sections. With size G hook, chain 5 sts. Sc in 2nd chain from hook and each ch across. Ch 1, turn (4 sts). Sc in each sc across. Ch 1, turn. Repeat until piece is 1 inch (2.5 cm) long.

2. Install a snap section on one of the squares. Insert the prongs through the fabric and the metal washer. Bend the prongs over the washer. Install the second snap on the other square.

3. Position the squares on the inside of the bag, near the upper edges at the center of each side. Sew them in place with matching yarn, catching the outer bag in the stitches.

CROCHETED CHENILLE

Soft chenille yarn, in variegated colors or brightened with a metallic strand, crochets quickly into a small, neat bag to give as a gift or wear to complement a special outfit. It's a great way to display a one-of-a-kind button, too.

The bag is simply a rectangle, folded in half and stitched up the sides. A button loop is added to the upper back edge. The shoulder strap can be made any length you wish. The finished bag is approximately 4-1/2 inches (11.5 cm) square.

Designer: AMY MOZINGO

MATERIALS

Chenille yarn, worsted weight, approximately 1-3/4 ounces (50 g)

Button, 3/4 inch (2 cm) diameter

Crochet hook, U.S. size F

INSTRUCTIONS

Crochet abbreviations are explained on page 59.

Gauge: sc, ch 1, sc, ch 1, sc, ch 1, sc, ch 1, sc equals 2 inches (5 cm). Four rows equal 1 inch (2.5 cm).

Row 1: Chain 29. Sc in 4th ch from hook. *Ch 1, skip 1 ch st, sc*; repeat to end of chain (13 sc plus first ch 3). Ch 3, turn.

Row 2: Sc in ch 1 space of previous row, *ch 1, sc in next space*, repeat to end of row.

Row 3 and on: Repeat row 2 until the piece is double the desired length. At the center of the last row make a chain approximately 13 sts long for the button loop. Join it to the bag at the starting point and finish the row.

Finishing

Fold the piece in half and line up the ch 1 holes on the sides. Working with two strands of yarn as one, sc through both ch 1 holes at the bottom of the bag. Ch 1, sc in next ch 1 space to the top of the bag. Continue the chain to make a strap the desired length. Sc in the ch 1 space at the top of the bag on opposite side. Work the side seam as before. Fasten off; weave in ends.

Position the button on the front of the purse so the loop will fit snugly. Sew the button with a smaller button behind it on the inside of the purse for reinforcement.

Designer: AMY MOZINGO

KNITTED
DAY-TO-EVENING BAG

A very proper little bag, with environmentally correct not-quite-tortoise handles, this one will take you from office to dinner in the best style. Add the optional crocheted strap to slip through the handles and over your shoulder—it's slim enough to tuck inside when it isn't needed. Worked in garter stitch, it's a breeze to knit, even for a novice.

The finished bag is 9 by 7 inches (22.5 by 17.5 cm), including handles. Ours is lined elegantly with black silk charmeuse.

Designers: JUDI ALWEIL AND ANNE RUBIN

MATERIALS

Rayon cordé, 144 yards (132 m)

D-shaped handles, 6 inches (15 cm) wide

Shank button, 5/8 inch (1.5 cm)

Crochet hook, U.S. size F

Needle, U.S. size 5

Lining fabric, 1/4 yard (.25 m)

Instructions

Crochet and knitting abbreviations are defined on page 59.

Front and back

Make two pieces.

Crochet 22 sc sts around bar of handle.

Row 1: With crochet hook, inc in every other st (total 33 sts).

Row 2: Work 1 row sc even.

Row 3: With knitting ndl, pick up 33 sts.

Row 4: Inc in every 5th st across. For a very even increase, pick up loop of stitch on needle (below the stitch) and put back on the left needle. Knit this stitch.

Work even in garter stitch (knit all rows) until piece measures 6 inches (15 cm).

Gusset

Cast on 6 sts. Work in garter st until approximately 20 1/2 inches (52 cm). It should fit around sides and bottom of bag. Put on a stitch holder.

Finishing

Beginning with the cast on edge of the gusset, whipstitch to one side of bag with right sides together, starting the gusset approximately 1/2 inch (1.5 cm) below the top of the bag. Work down the side, across the bottom, and up the other side, ending the same distance from the top as you began. Adjust the gusset length to fit; bind off. Sew on the other section.

Button loop

Attach the cord just below the handle on the center back. Crochet a chain approximately 3 inches (7.5 cm) long. Fold in half and slip stitch end to beginning point. Sew the button on the outside of the bag front.

Shoulder strap

Attach cord to top of side gusset. Chain 45 inches (114 cm), or desired length. Attach with slip stitch to other side of gusset. Slip stitch back to the beginning of the chain and fasten off.

Lining

Fold the lining fabric in half. Place the bag on the fabric, smoothing it flat, and chalk mark around the edges, marking the upper edge at the lower edge of the handles. Even up the lines, and add 1/2 inch (1.5 cm) hem allowance at the top. Because of the difference between the inner and outer bag dimensions, it isn't necessary to add seam allowance. Cut out the pieces.

Add a pocket to one or both sides of the lining if desired. Stitch the lining with right sides together, and fit it into the bag. Fold under the hem at the upper edge to just below the topmost row of stitches (there should be a little ease). Whipstitch to the bag along the fold.

CROCHETED PATCHWORK BAG

Granny's squares were never quite like this! Rayon raffia yarn and vivid colors team up in a great summer bag to travel with you everywhere.

The bag closes with a magnetic snap hidden under a crocheted flap. For security, it is lined with fabric to match the background color—or to contrast, if you prefer. The bag is 10 inches (25.5 cm) square, with a 35-inch (89-cm) strap.

MATERIALS AND TOOLS
Rayon raffia yarn, 72-yard (68-m) skeins: 3 of background color (MC), 1 each of hot pink (A), orange (B), yellow gold (C), and red (D)

Magnetic snap, 3/4 inch (2 cm) diameter

Crochet hook, U.S. size F

Yarn needle

Lining fabric, 3/8 yard (.35 m)

INSTRUCTIONS
For crochet abbreviations, see page 59.

Front and back
Make 19 squares: make 9 in color combination 1, and 10 in combination 2 (the odd one will be the flap).

Combination 1:
Foundation chain: (color A) chain 6, join with sl st to form a ring.

Rnd 1: (A) ch 3, 2 dc, ch 3, *3 dc, ch 3 into ring.* Repeat between ** twice; join with sl st.

Rnd 2: (B) sl st to first space, (ch 3, 2 dc, ch 3, 3 dc) into 1st ch 3 space, *ch 1, 3 dc into ch 1 space, (ch 1, 3 dc, ch 3, 3 dc) into each corner.* Repeat between **, ending with ch 1; join with a sl st.

Rnd 3: (MC) sl st to 1st space, (ch 2, 2 dc, ch 3, 3 dc) into 1st ch 3 space, *ch 1, 3 dc into ch 1 space, (ch 1, 3 dc, ch 3, 3 dc) into each corner.* Repeat between **, end with ch 1; join with sl st. End off.

Combination 2:
Substitute color C for A, and D for B in the directions above.

Assembly
For each side, lay out the squares in a checkerboard pattern, using the photo as a guide. Using the raffia, whipstitch the squares together. Work sc around the edges.

Lightly steam press the pieces, using a pressing cloth. Ease them into shape and allow to dry completely.

Whipstitch the pieces together on three sides. Work 1 row sc around the opening.

Flap
With the remaining combination 2 square and MC yarn:

Work 18 sc along the last row of the square, ch 1, turn.

Row 2: work 18 sc, ch 1; turn.

Row 3: work 18 sc, ch 3; turn.

Row 4: hdc in back of 18 sc.

Whipstitch flap to the top middle square in the matching color combination.

Shoulder strap
Attach raffia to the top of the bag at the side seam. Chain approximately 38 inches (96 cm), making sure to keep the chain flat. Attach at the opposite side with a sl st. Sl stitch back in each ch and attach to beginning point with a sl st.

Lining
A lining will keep the bag's interior neat, and allows for the addition of a pocket or two for small items.

1. Fold the lining fabric piece in half, lengthwise. Place the finished bag on the fabric with one side along the fold, and smooth it flat. Chalk mark the outline of the bag. At the top, add 1 inch (2.5 cm) for a hem.

2. Straighten the lines and cut. There is no need to add seam allowance—the difference in the inner and outer dimensions of the bag will allow for the seams.

3. Add a pocket if you wish (see page 5 for suggestions).

4. Stitch across the bottom and up the side using approximately 1/4 inch (.5 cm) seam allowance.

5. Fit the lining into the bag; there should be a little ease. Fold under the upper edge to approximately 3/8 inch (1 cm) below the top of the bag. Whipstitch in place.

Magnetic snap

1. Crochet two reinforcement pieces to place behind the snap sections. Chain 5 sts. Sc in 2nd chain from hook and each ch across. Ch 1, turn (4 sts). Sc in each sc across. Ch 1, turn. Repeat until piece is 1 inch (2.5 cm) long.

2. Install one part of the snap in a crocheted square by inserting the prongs through the square and the metal washer. Bend the prongs over the washer.

3. Position the piece on the underside of the flap and sew it in place with raffia.

4. Attach the other snap section on the remaining square. Sew it to the outside of the bag front, positioning it to allow a little ease so the bag will close neatly when it is filled.

Designers: JUDI ALWEIL AND ANNE RUBIN

Designer: Amy Mozingo

Silk Purse

It is crocheted not with yarn, but with strips of fabric from an old, worn silk sari. The resulting fabric is very soft and dense, the fine threads from the raw edges of the strips contributing to its distinctive texture.

If you don't have a source for old saris, fabric yardage will work just as well. Fine, tightly woven material works best. The tighter the weave, the narrower the strips can be cut. You might wish to try painting your own yardage for some exciting color effects.

To get a feel for the technique, experiment first with strips of your fabric. Cut strips on the fabric straight grain, 1/4 to 1/2 inch (.7 to 1.3 cm) wide, to find the optimum width for your particular material. Mark the strips into one-yard increments and crochet a gauge swatch in order to estimate the required yardage and the best hook size to use.

Work with the longest strips you can cut. With lengths shorter than approximately 2 feet (.65 m), a great deal of time will be spent adding new strips.

When you join on a new strip, don't knot the two—the knot will invariably work its way to the right side, and the knots will produce a lumpy fabric. Instead, just overlap the ends approximately 2 inches (5 cm) and work them together as a single strand for several stitches.

PURSE WITH TOP OPENING

This purse consists of a long rectangle, folded in half and stitched up the sides. Two buttonholes are worked near one end. The finished size will vary according to materials used but should be approximately 4 to 5-1/2 inches (10 to 14 cm) wide. Make the total length of the piece slightly more than double the width.

MATERIALS

    Silk strips, according to gauge

    Crochet hook, U.S. size J, or the size that
        works with your fabric

    2 buttons, 3/4 inch (2 cm) diameter

INSTRUCTIONS

Crochet abbreviations are explained on page 59.

Gauge: sc, ch 1, sc, ch 1, sc, ch 1, sc, ch 1, sc equals 2 inches (5 cm). Four rows equal 1 inch (2.5 cm).

Row 1: Chain 29. Sc in 4th ch from hook. *Ch 1, skip 1 ch st, sc*; repeat to end of chain (13 sc plus first ch 3). Ch 3, turn.

Row 2: Sc in ch 1 space of previous row, *ch 1, sc in next space*, repeat to end of row.

Row 3 and on: Repeat row 2 until the piece is 1 inch (2.5 cm) short of double the desired length.

Buttonholes

Each buttonhole is approximately 1 inch (2.5 cm) wide.

Buttonhole row 1: Begin the row as usual but crochet only 2 sc then, instead of ch 1, ch 5. Skip the next 2 ch 1 spaces. Sc/ch 1 as usual 5 times. SC, ch 5, skip the next 2 ch 1 spaces, sc. Finish row as usual.

Buttonhole row 2: Crochet as usual, putting 3 (sc/ch 1) in the spaces formed by the ch 5 on previous row. Repeat row 2 until desired length is reached.

Finishing

Fold the piece in half and line up the ch 1 spaces on the sides. Treating two fabric strands as one, sc through both ch 1 spaces at bottom of the bag. Ch 1, sc in next ch 1 space, to the top of the bag. Continue the chain to make a strap of the desired length. Sc in the ch 1 space at the top of the bag on the other side. Then join the sides of the bag as before. Fasten off the strand and weave in the end.

Sew buttons onto the inside back of the purse opposite the buttonholes. Use strong thread and try to hide the stitches so they won't be noticeable on the outside of the bag.

PURSE WITH FLAP

Plan the flap length at about 2/3 the length of the bag front. Follow the instructions above, but make just one buttonhole, centering it approximately 1 inch (2.5 cm) from the end of the flap. Sew the button to the purse front with a small button behind it on the inside of the purse as reinforcement.

A BASKETWEAVE BAG TO KNIT

Its light, delicate appearance is deceiving, because this compact little bag is actually quite sturdy. At 6 by 8 inches (15 by 20.5 cm), the size is just right, too. It's large enough to hold the everyday essentials comfortably, and still small enough to go out for the evening.

The bag shown here has a decorative "tortoise shell" ornament concealing the magnetic catch. An alternative closure—a silky tassel, big bright button, or antique brooch—would completely change the character of the bag.

Consider the lining fabric, too. Elegant silk shantung, bright cotton plaid, or your design stenciled onto crisp cotton—any one of them would be perfectly appropriate and each would create its own unique effect.

Designers: JUDI ALWEIL AND ANNE RUBIN

MATERIALS

- Knitting needles, U.S. size 5
- Crochet hook, U.S. sizes G and F
- Yarn needle
- Rayon soutache or rayon cordé yarn, approximately 144 yards
- Fabric for lining, 3/8 yard (.35 m)
- Magnetic snap or other closure
- Ornament for bag flap

INSTRUCTIONS

Knitting gauge is not the critical issue with a bag that it would be with a garment. If you use other than the suggested yarn, however, knit several inches of the pattern the full width of the bag back to check your gauge against the measurements above.

Front and back

Make two pieces.

On no. 5 needles, cast on 32 sts.

Row 1: K4, P4 across row, ending with P4.

Row 2: K4, P4 across row, ending with P4.

Rows 3-6: Repeat these 2 rows 2 times (6 rows).

Row 7: P4, K4 across row ending with K4.

Row 8: P4, K4 across row ending with K4.

Rows 9-12: Repeat these 2 rows 2 times (6 rows)

Repeat this 12-row pattern until piece measures 8 inches (20 cm).

Work one row sc on right side along sides and bottom of each piece. Slip stitch the pieces together on the wrong side.

Flap

On the back piece with the right side facing, pick up 32 sts. Knit first 10 rows of pattern. Working in pattern, dec 1 st each side every other tow until 24 sts remain. There should be a total of 18 rows. Bind off around the flap. Weave in all ends.

Crocheted or twisted cord strap

For a crocheted strap: Join cord to one edge of the bag at the seam. With size G hook, Ch 141. Keeping ch untwisted, sl st to second edge of bag at seam. *Ch 1, sl st in next ch; repeat from * across; sl st to bag edge

then rep from * across opposite side of the strap. At the end, sl st to bag edge and fasten off. Weave in loose ends.

For a twisted cord strap: Make a twisted cord the desired length, using three strands of yarn. To measure cord, double the desired finished length and add 2 feet (.65 m). Secure one end of the group of strands, hold them taut from the other end, and twist them together evenly. Fold the cord in half and allow it to twist back on itself. Tie a double overhand knot about 2 inches (5 cm) from each end of the cord. Trim the ends evenly and stitch to the inside of the bag.

Magnetic closure

Crochet a small square to reinforce behind the snap on the underside of the flap. With a size F hook, chain 5 sts. Sc in 2nd chain from hook and each ch across (4 sts). Ch 1, turn. Sc in each sc across. Ch 1, turn. Repeat until piece is 1 inch (2.5 cm) long. Install one half of the magnetic latch in the crocheted piece by inserting the prongs through the fabric and the metal washer. Bend the prongs over the washer. Position the crocheted piece on the inside of the flap and sew in place with a strand of the bag yarn. Position the other half of the snap on the outer front of the bag, allowing a little ease, and assemble as before.

Lining

A pretty lining not only makes the bag look better, but in the case of a knitted or crocheted bag helps it retain its shape.

1. Fold the lining fabric piece in half, lengthwise. Place the finished bag on the fabric with one side along the fold, and smooth it flat. Chalk mark the outline of the bag.

2. Straighten the lines and cut. There is no need to add seam allowance—the difference in the inner and outer dimensions of the bag will allow for the seams.

3. Add a pocket if you wish.

4. Stitch across the bottom and up the side using approximately 1/4 inch (.5 cm) seam allowance.

5. Fit the lining into the bag; there should be a little ease. Fold under the edge to approximately 3/8 inch (1 cm) below the top of the bag.

CHAPTER 5

SPECIAL-OCCASION BAGS

Certain events call for an out-of-the-ordinary sort of bag. It need only hold the essentials for a festive evening. It must serve as the perfect accessory for your most glamorous outfit—yet not compete for attention. For just such occasions, the small purses shown in this chapter offer lots of promise. Each design has many possible variations, and all of them are suitably distinctive.

LAMÉ-LINED SILK

The design is actually very simple; it's the fabric that is exotic. A beautiful piece of striped Indian silk is used for the outer shell and lightweight lamé for the lining. The combination is glamorous enough for the most festive evening you can imagine.

The bag and lining are just circles, shaped at the outer edges and provided with a casing for the drawstring. Opened up, it is 17-1/2 inches (44.5 cm) in diameter.

MATERIALS

Fabric for the shell: an 18-inch (46-cm) square

Fabric for the lining, the same size

Rayon rattail cord or jeweler's cord: 2 1/4 yards (2.1 m)

Paper and tape for pattern making

INSTRUCTIONS

1. Make a paper pattern. On a large sheet of paper, draw a circle 13 inches (33 cm) in diameter. Draw an equilateral triangle 3-3/4 inches (9.5 cm) on a side, and cut ten of these from paper.

2. Tape the triangles around the perimeter of the paper circle with the points of the bases just touching. Cut the shell and lining fabrics from the pattern.

3. Work two buttonholes, 1/2 inch (1.3 cm) long, on the shell fabric. Position them opposite each other on the piece, at the base of a triangle, the outer end of each 1/2 inch (1.3 cm) from the fabric edge.

4. Sew the shell to the lining with right sides together, using 1/4 inch (.7 cm) seam allowance, and leaving open along the side of a triangle for turning. Trim the outer points and clip the seam allowance at the inner points. Turn; press flat.

5. Stitch the cord casing. Chalk mark a circle 1/4 inch (.7 cm) inside the inner points of the triangles, at the outer ends of the buttonholes. Pin the layers together, and stitch around the marked line. Stitch again 1/2 inch (1.3 cm) inside the first stitching line.

6. Cut the cord in two. With a bodkin or safety pin, thread one length into the casing through one of the buttonholes, around the bag, and back out at the same point. Knot the ends together. Thread the other cord from the other buttonhole.

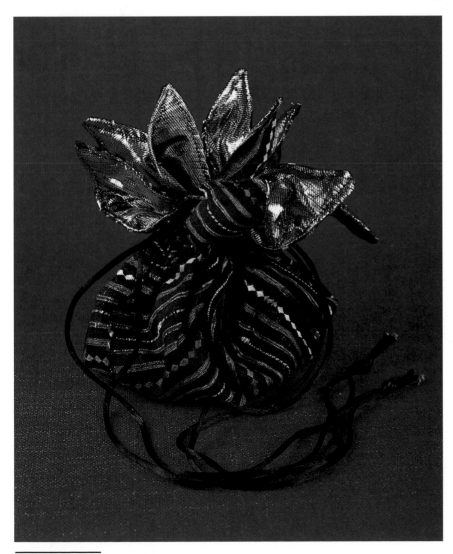

Designer: **AMY MOZINGO**

Designer: **LORI KERR**

ALMOST BASIC BLACK BAG

The floral appliqué alone is pretty enough, but it is the stitched accents that make this evening bag a true work of art. The flowers and leaves are given dimension and detail with stitching worked in shimmery rayon thread, in shades slightly darker than the fabric colors. Bright metallic thread provides the highlights.

Both the bag and lining are soft rayon/cotton moiré, with thick rayon cord for the strap and a finer cord for the drawstring. Purchased tassels at the corners add a festive note. The appliqué fabric is cotton, in soft watercolor hues. The bag is 8-1/2 inches (21.5 cm) wide and 13 inches (33 cm) high.

MATERIALS

Fabric, for bag and lining: 1/2 yard (.5 m), 45 inches (115 cm) wide

Cord for the strap: 1-1/4 yards (1.15 m)

Cord for the drawstring: 2/3 yard (.65 m)

Fabric scraps for appliqué

Paper-backed fusible web, light weight

Three tassels

Decorative rayon threads for appliqué

Metallic thread

INSTRUCTIONS

Seam allowance is 1/2 inch (1.3 cm)

1. For the bag front and back, cut two rectangles 9-1/2 inches (24 cm) wide and 15 inches (38 cm) long. For the lining, cut two pieces the same width and 13 inches (33 cm) long.

2. Shape the bottom of the bag. Stack the four pieces with sides and lower edges aligned. Mark the center of the lower edge. On the sides, mark a spot 1-1/2 inches (4 cm) above each lower corner. Connect the marks with chalk lines and cut along the lines.

3. Work buttonholes for the drawstring on the bag front. Mark the center front, 3 inches (7.5 cm) below the upper edge of the bag. Draw a line at this point, parallel with the bag edge and about an inch to either side of center. Work two vertical 1/2-inch (1.3-cm) buttonholes approximately 1 inch (2.5 cm) apart, the upper ends at the marked line.

4. Enlarge the appliqué patterns.

5. Apply backing to the appliqué fabrics according to the manufacturer's instructions. Trace the designs onto the paper backing and cut out the motifs. Using the photo as a guide, layer the pieces and apply them to the bag front.

6. With rayon thread, stitch around the edges of the motifs and add details. Use the metallic thread for accents.

7. Pin a tassel to the bag front right side at each lower corner, the fringe toward the center of the bag. Stitch the back to the front with right sides together along the sides and bottom. Trim, and press.

8. Stitch the lining sections in the same way, leaving an opening between two bottom corners.

9. With right sides together, place the bag inside the lining. Align the upper edges and stitch. Turn right side out through the opening, then slipstitch it closed. Work the lining well into the bag; the outer bag will fold approximately 1 inch (2.5 cm) to the inside. Press the edge.

10. Chalk mark the casing stitching lines just above and below the buttonholes, keeping the lines parallel with the bag edge. Stitch along the lines. Thread the cord through the casing.

11. Position the strap ends at the side seamlines, the ends slightly below the lower casing stitching line. Stitch securely across each end twice, just above and again just below the casing stitching lines.

MOTIFS FOR LILY AND LEAVES APPLIQUÉ. ENLARGE 200%.

QUILTED OCTAGON

A piece of trapunto-stitched cotton upholstery fabric inspired the design for this very refined little purse. The stitching, worked with thread to match the fabric, adds dimension in a subtle way. Because the bag is open at the top, the same fabric color was used for the lining.

The outer fabric is quilted to a layer of batting, offering a perfect opportunity to experiment with free-motion quilting on a small scale. Detailed instructions for this technique are on page 14. The bag is 6-3/4 inches (17 cm) wide and 5-1/2 inches (14 cm) high.

MATERIALS

Fabric for bag: 1/4 yard (.25 m)

Lining fabric: 1/4 yard (.25 m)

Fusible garment-weight batting, if the bag will be quilted: 1/4 yard (.25 m)

Stiff fusible interfacing, if the bag will not be quilted: 1/4 yard (.25 m)

Decorative cord: 3-1/2 yards (3.2 m)

Two large clear snaps

Designer: JOYCE BALDWIN

INSTRUCTIONS

Seam allowance is 1/2 inch (1.3 cm) except as noted.

If the bag will be quilted, cut outer fabric and batting slightly larger than the pattern pieces to allow for shrinkage caused by the stitching. Trim to the pattern after stitching.

1. Enlarge the pattern and cut it from paper.

2. Use the pattern to cut two pieces each of outer fabric, lining, and batting or interfacing.

3. Cut one gusset section, 3-1/4 by 16 inches (8.5 by 40.5 cm), from outer fabric and from lining. Cut a strip of interfacing or batting the same length and 1 inch (2.5 cm) wide.

4. Cut the cord into two 41-inch (104-cm) lengths for the straps and two 13-1/2-inch (34-cm) lengths for the edging. If cord ravels easily, use hand stitches wrapped several times around the cord before cutting to the required lengths.

5. For a quilted bag, fuse batting to the bag front and back pieces. On the gusset, apply the batting between the center and one seamline of the strip.

6. Stitch the bag front and back in the pattern of your choice (the gusset will be stitched after it is assembled). Trim the pieces to match the lining. Trim batting to the seamlines.

7. If the bag will not be quilted, trim seam allowances from the interfacing pieces and apply them to the bag front and back pieces, following the manufacturer's instructions. On the gusset, apply the interfacing between the center and one seamline of the strip.

8. If you wish, add a pocket to the back lining, placing it as shown on the pattern.

9. Pin bag back and lining with right sides together. Insert ends of the strap cord between the layers at the large dots, the ends at the fabric edges. Stitch around seven sides, leaving the seam open between the small dots at the bottom and keeping the cord free. Assemble the front piece in the same way. Grade seam allowances.

10. Turn the pieces right side out through the openings. Turn under the seam allowances at the openings, press, and slipstitch closed. Press all seam edges to flatten them.

11. Fold the gusset in half lengthwise, right sides together, and stitch the long seam. Turn right side out; press. Quilt through all layers with evenly spaced rows of stitching. Clean finish the ends. Fold under 1-1/4 inches (3 cm) at one end of the gusset and press.

12. Position the folded end of the gusset at the marked triangle on one front or back section. Using doubled thread, hand stitch the gusset to the bag piece. Continue around the bottom of the bag and up to the marked triangle at the other side. Fold under the end of the gusset at the triangle; press. Stitch the other bag section in place. Slipstitch the gusset ends to the lining.

13. Beginning at the upper end of the gusset on one side, fold approximately 1 inch (2.5 cm) of cord into the bag. Hand stitch the end in place, and stitch the cord all the way around the seamline on the outside of the bag, then across the top in front of the straps, ending where you began. Stitch the remaining cord around the other seamline in the same way.

14. Sew the snaps to the bag lining below the ends of the straps.

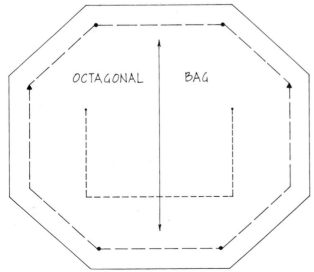

PATTERN, OCTAGONAL BAG FRONT/BACK. ENLARGE 255%.

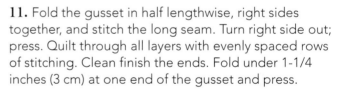

A Sampler of Techniques

A simple envelope, zipped across the top, provides a perfect setting for stitching experiments and explorations. And the result? An evening bag with two different faces, each unique.

Three pieces of "fabric" were constructed especially for the bag, then sewn together with tiny corded piping to define the seamlines. On the front, metallic print material was tucked, then embroidered with decorative thread to keep the tucks in place. The bottom of the bag is silk, the stripes embroidered with another decorative thread. And the third fabric, on the back, is solid-colored satin, lines of double-needle stitching added with contrasting thread.

Almost any decorative techniques could be incorporated into this design. In addition to embroidery, painted or stenciled fabric might be used. A beaded design could be applied to one of the pieces. A section could be smocked. A cutwork design might be added, or some appliqué. There is just no limit to the combinations that are possible.

The bag has a traditional lining and a strap of purchased cord. It is 8-1/2 inches (20.5 cm) wide and 8 inches (20 cm) long.

Designer: **Lori Kerr**

MATERIALS

Assorted fabrics for the bag, according to the design

Lining fabric: 9-1/2 inches (24 cm) wide and 17 inches (43 cm) long

Narrow piping cord: 1/2 yard (.5 m)

Zipper: 9-inch (23-cm) length

Lightweight fusible interfacing: 1/4 yard (.25 m)

Decorative cord for strap: 1-1/4 yards (1.15 m) or as needed

Decorative threads for embellishment

Optional but handy: fabric pleater

INSTRUCTIONS

Cut the lining fabric first and use it as a guide for size and placement of the outer fabrics.

Creating the fabrics

1. For the tucked section, start with a rectangle the width of the lining and approximately 15 inches (38 cm) long. Allow 1/2 inch (1.3 cm) at each end and pleat the fabric horizontally. Use a canvas fabric pleater, if you have one, to form the pleats. Otherwise, work one pleat at a time from the upper edge of the piece. On the right side of the fabric, press horizontal tucks along the fabric grain, spacing them 1/4 inch (.7 cm), or so, apart. The finished piece should be 5-1/2 inches (14 cm) long.

2. When the tucks are pressed in place, apply lightweight interfacing to the wrong side of the piece to hold them. Then stitch a random pattern on the right side with decorative thread.

3. For the striped fabric, simply work vertical lines of stitching at intervals with a decorative thread. On this fabric, a very soft silk, the stitching puckered the fabric slightly, adding a shirred effect that was unplanned but most welcome. Trim the fabric to the width of the lining and 7-1/2 inches (19 cm) in length.

4. For the third fabric, use a twin or triple needle with contrasting thread, perhaps to match one of the other fabrics. Trim the finished piece to the lining width and 6-1/2 inches (16.5 cm) long.

5. Wrap the piping cord with a bias fabric strip approximately 1-1/2 inches (4 cm) wide. Stitch close to the cord. Cut the piece in half.

Assembly

Seam allowance is 1/2 inch (1.3 cm) except as noted.

1. Join the fabrics. Stitch the three pieces end to end, with right sides together, incorporating piping in each seam. Trim the piece, if necessary, to match the lining.

2. Install the zipper. Fold the piece wrong side out, ends aligned. Baste the seam and press it open. Center the zipper along the seam, face down on the wrong side of the fabric. Stitch both sides and across the ends.

3. Open the zipper. Fold the bag, right sides together, with the zipper at the top. Position a strap end at each side, approximately 1 inch (2.5 cm) below the upper edge of the bag, the ends of the cord aligned with the bag edges. Stitch the side seams. Stitch back and forth across the cord ends in the seam allowance.

4. Square the lower corners to give the bag depth. With the bag wrong side out, fold each lower corner to create a point at the lower end of the seam. Stitch across the point approximately 1 inch (2.5 cm) from the end of the seam, stitching exactly perpendicular to the seamline as shown in the drawing on page 9. Trim; press.

5. Make the lining. Fold the piece in half crosswise, right sides together. Stitch the side seams. Form points at the lower corners as for the bag. Press under the seam allowance at the raw edges. Place the lining in the bag and slipstitch the pressed edges to the zipper tape.

TEARDROP BAG FOR EVENING

The generously sized shoulder bag shown on pages 26-32 scales down neatly for occasions when you don't need to carry every important thing you own. The little bag is quite capacious despite its glamorous appearance.

This one is made of crushed velvet, decorated with free-motion stitching worked in glittering metallic thread. A fringe of beads is stitched along the seamline at the lower edge. For the strap, a stuffed fabric tube is wound with a strand of thread. A tassel made of the decorative thread makes a festive zipper pull.

The bag is 11 inches (28 cm) long and 6 inches (15 cm) wide across the lower end.

Designer: **LORI KERR**

MATERIALS

Fabric for the bag: 1/2 yard (.5 m)

Lining fabric: 3/8 yard (.35 m)

Cool-fuse interfacing: 3/8 yard (.35 m)

Bugle beads and seed beads

Metallic thread to match the fabric

Soft cording, 1/2 inch (1.3 cm) diameter: 2-1/2 yards (2.3 m)

INSTRUCTIONS

Seam allowance is 3/8 inch (1 cm) except as noted.

1. Enlarge the pattern and zipper gusset guide and cut them from paper.

2. Cut two bag sections and two of interfacing by the solid lines of the pattern. Cut two lining sections, cutting at the dotted line indicating the lining extension. For the zipper gusset, cut two pieces from the bag fabric, 3-1/4 by 8 inches (8 by 20 cm). From the bag fabric, cut two 3-1/4-inch (8 cm) squares. For the strap, cut a strip 45 inches (115 cm) long and 2 inches (5 cm) wide.

3. Apply interfacing to the wrong sides of the bag pieces following the manufacturer's instructions.

4. Decorate the pieces with free-motion stitching (instructions are on page 14), keeping within the seamlines.

5. Install the zipper. Fold the two fabric rectangles in half lengthwise, right side out; press the folds. With the zipper right side up, place one folded edge along the stitching line on the zipper tape. Stitch close to the fold. Stitch the other fabric piece to the other side of the zipper.

6. Press under the seam allowance on one side of each fabric square. Position the folded edge of one square across each end of the zipper, just beyond the teeth and with the fold perpendicular to the zipper. Stitch close to the fold.

7. Use the guide to trim the finished zipper gusset to size. Transfer the marked dots.

8. Make the strap. Fold the strip in half lengthwise, wrong side out. Stitch the long edges, using 1/4 inch (.5 cm) seam allowance. Insert an end of the cord into the end of the tube, and stitch across the end through the cord. Turn the tube right side out, pulling the cord through. Cut off the excess cord, and cut away the cord from the seam allowances at the ends of the tube.

9. Thread a needle with the metallic thread and knot it securely at one end of the tube. Wrap it tightly around the length of the tube in a spiral pattern. Knot at the other end.

10. With right sides together, stitch the bag back and front around the curved edge, leaving open along the zipper gusset seamline.

11. Baste the ends of the strap at the seamlines at the open edge, the ends even with the edge of the bag.

12. Open the zipper. Pin the zipper gusset into the opening, right sides together. Stitch.

13. Make the lining. Stitch the sections with right sides together, beginning and ending at the stitching line on the extension edge. Press under the seam allowances along the opening.

14. Place the lining in the bag. By hand, stitch the folded edges along the zipper tape.

15. Add beaded fringe along the curved section of the seam. Take several stitches along the seam, then string some beads. Bring the needle back up through all but the last bead on the strand, and take several more stitches into the bag seam. Add the desired number of strands this same way, making them shorter toward the ends of the seam.

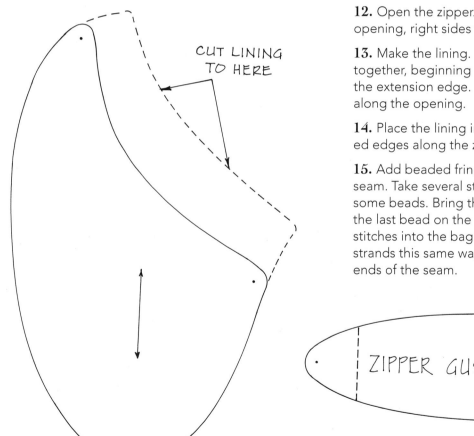

CUT LINING TO HERE

ZIPPER GUSSET GUIDE

Teardrop Evening Bag: pattern for bag and lining (left) and zipper gusset guide (right). Enlarge both pieces 286%.

Tapestry Semicircle

Designer: LORI KERR

Elegant tapestry fabric needs little in the way of ornamentation to create a very special bag. This fabric is upholstery weight, an interior designer's sample. The button on the flap is strictly ornamental—a hook and loop tape "button" under the flap actually does the work. Decorative cord edges the flap, then continues as the shoulder strap.

The bag is 6-1/2 inches (16.5 cm) wide and 4-1/2 inches (11.5 cm) high.

MATERIALS

Fabric for the bag: 1/4 yard (.25 m)

Lining fabric: 1/4 yard

Decorative cord, 1/8 inch (.3 cm) diameter: 1-3/4 yards (1.6 m)

Button

Small piece of hook and loop tape

Purchased or custom-made tassel

INSTRUCTIONS

1. From the bag fabric, cut a rectangle 7-1/2 inches (19 cm) wide and 8-1/2 inches (21.5 cm) long. Cut a second rectangle the same width, 5 inches (13 cm) long.

2. Cut lining pieces the same sizes.

3. Stack the pieces with the long edges and lower short edges aligned. Fold lengthwise then crosswise into fourths, aligning the corners. Use a cup or other round object as a template to round the corners of the bag lower edge and flap. Chalk mark the line, then cut through all layers.

4. Sew the bag pieces, right sides together, around the curved sides and bottom.

5. Sew the lining front and back the same way, but leave an opening at the bottom for turning.

6. Place the bag inside the lining, right sides together, and stitch the bag to the lining around the opening and flap. Clip into the seam allowance at the corners of the bag back/flap. Trim; press. Turn right side out.

7. Press under the seam allowances along the lining opening. Overlap them just slightly. Stitch along the fold, through the lining and bag, on the bag seamline, closing the opening at the same time.

8. Position the cord to check the strap length before you stitch. Knot the cord approximately 1 inch (2.5 cm) from each end. Place one end inside the bag at the side seamline, the knot at the upper edge. Pin the cord around the flap edge to the other side seamline. Start the other cord end at the opposite side of the bag in the same way and pin it around to the side with the first cord end. There should now be a double row of cord around the flap edge, with the remainder forming a loop for the strap.

9. If the strap length is correct, unpin the inner cord around the flap and stitch the outer one in place with a cording foot and zigzag stitch, or using the blind hem foot and a narrow stitch width setting to just catch the edge of the cord. Replace the inner row of cord, tight against the first row, and stitch it. Stitch the knots securely to the side seams.

10. Stitch hook and loop tape to the underside of the flap and to the bag front. Sew the ornamental button onto the flap. Add a tassel—use a purchased one or make your own; instructions are on page 6.

CHAPTER 6

DISPLAY YOUR ARTISTRY

Whatever your favorite studio sport, a bag provides a practical way to show it off. Almost any kind of needlework can be applied to a handbag in one way or another. The collection of bags on the following pages includes some techniques that may be familiar to you, along with a few that you may have always wanted to try.

Designs from Nature

The colors and motifs of all the seasons are combined in a bag that's as practical to use as it is pretty to look at. The front of the bag is pieced, with strips and small squares of several cotton prints that work nicely together. The back and flap are cotton damask. The outer and lining fabrics are quilted to a thin batting using free-motion stitching—this designer's specialty.

To decorate the flap, a motif cut from one of the prints is held in place with several rows of straight stitching. Seed beads are sprinkled here and there for a touch of sparkle. For the closure, a fabric strip sewn to the flap simply wraps around the toggle button. The bag is approximately 8-1/2 inches (21.5) wide and 9 inches (23 cm) long, with a 38-inch (96-cm) strap.

Materials

- Fabric for the bag back and flap: a rectangle approximately 10 by 15 inches (25.5 by 38 cm)
- Fabric scraps to piece for the bag front
- Lining fabric: 3/8 yard (.35 m)
- Garment-weight batting or cotton flannel: 3/8 yard (.35 m)
- Complementary fabric for binding, strap, and appliqué, approximately 1/4 yard (.25 m)
- Button
- Optional: small seed beads

Designer: **Karen Swing**

INSTRUCTIONS

Quilting will cause the fabrics to draw up slightly, so pieces will be cut slightly larger than needed and will be trimmed to size later. Allow for this when planning a design. If you haven't tried free-motion quilting, read the tips on page 14.

Cutting

1. Cut lining and batting for the bag front 10 inches (25.5 cm) wide and 9-1/2 inches (24 cm) long.

2. For the back/flap section, cut lining and batting 10 by 15 inches (25.5 by 38 cm).

3. For the strap, cut a strip 2 inches (5 cm) wide and 39 inches (99 cm) long on the lengthwise fabric grain.

4. Cut a strip for the button loop 1-1/2 inches (4 cm) wide and 6 inches (15.5 cm) long.

5. To bind the opening and flap, cut a strip on the bias or crossgrain, 2 inches (5 cm) wide and 24 inches (61 cm) long.

Piecing and quilting

1. Piece fabric scraps to the size of the front lining.

2. Layer the pieced section and lining right sides out and sandwich the batting between. Pin baste. To stabilize the fabric for stitching, spray starch one side of the piece, allow it to dry, then starch the other side.

3. Quilt the layers, using the free-motion technique.

4. Layer the back/flap sections and quilt them together.

5. Cut a motif from a fabric scrap and appliqué to the flap front. Add beads if desired, or add other decorative stitching.

6. Trim the bag front to 9-1/2 inches (24 cm) wide and 9 inches (22.5 cm) long. Trim the back/flap to the same width, 13-1/2 inches (34 cm) long.

Assembly

1. Make the strap. Sew the long edges of the strip, right sides together, using 1/4-inch (.7-cm) seam allowance. Trim, turn and press. Alternatively, press in half, right side out, then press the raw edges in to the center fold. Stitch along both edges.

2. Stitch the button strip in the same way.

3. Place the bag front and back with right sides together and lower edges aligned. Stitch the side seams using 1/2 inch (1/5 cm) seam allowance. Trim, and overcast the seams neatly.

4. Stitch across the lower corners to give the bag depth. With the bag wrong side out, fold each lower corner to form a point as shown in the drawing on page 9. Stitch across, approximately 1 inch (2.5 cm) from the end of the seam, stitching exactly perpendicular to the side seamline. Trim and overcast.

5. Trim the sides of the flap so they are slightly narrower than the finished front of the bag as shown. On each side, make a cut, approximately 3/4 inch (2 cm), straight back from the top of the side seamline, then straight up each side of the flap. Round the inner corners slightly, as shown in the illustration on page 11.

6. Position a strap end at each side, the ends aligned with the bag upper edge. Stitch securely in the seam allowance.

7. Baste one end of the button strip at the center of the flap front, the end even with the flap edge.

8. With right sides together and beginning on the front, stitch the binding strip to the bag with edges aligned, using 3/8 inch (1 cm) seam allowance. At the flap/front corners, ease the fabric and clip into the seam allowances as necessary. Fold under the overlapping end. Press binding toward the seam allowances. Trim.

9. Fold under the raw edge of the strip so the fold just covers the previous stitching line and stitch by hand, or stitch in the ditch from the right side.

10. Knot the free end of the button strip, incorporating a bead if you wish. Sew the button to the bag front.

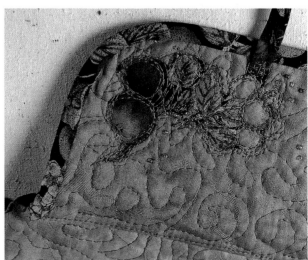

SMOCKED TURTLENECK BAG

An elegant small handbag for smocking enthusiasts is worked in silk dupioni and embellished with seed beads. Creative pleating gives the bag its shape—the fabric piece is pleated both horizontally and vertically. Smocking around the base of the collar creates a channel for a drawstring of twisted cord made from strands of embroidery floss. The bottom of the bag is stabilized with an inner layer of plastic needlepoint mesh and edged at the seamline with fine corded piping.

MATERIALS AND TOOLS

- Fabric, for bag and lining: 3/4 yard (.7 m)
- Seed beads: two tubes
- Hand sewing needle: an embroidery or milliner's needle that will pass through beads
- Thread: embroidery floss, floche, machine silk, or other thread to fit needle
- Fine piping cord: 1/2 yard (.5 m)
- Needlepoint plastic: two 4-inch (10-cm) circles
- Decorative cord for drawstring: 1 yard (1 m)
- Bodkin or large tapestry needle
- Liquid fray retardant
- Smocking pleater and thread

INSTRUCTIONS

Seam allowances of 1/2 inch (1.3 cm) are included. For the outer bag side seam, seam allowance will be figured after the pleating is finished.

Cutting

For the outer bag, cut a rectangle 25 inches (63.5 cm) by 18 inches (46 cm) long. For the lining, cut a rectangle 18 inches (46 cm) wide and 6-1/2 inches (16.5 cm) long. For the bottom of the bag, cut a 5-inch (12.5-cm) circle from outer fabric and from lining. Cut a bias strip of outer fabric 1 inch (2.5 cm) wide and 15 inches (38 cm) long for the piping.

Preparing to pleat

To make the ten smocked stripes in the body of the bag, the fabric must go through a 16-row pleater three times; through a 24-row pleater, twice. Because the fabric must be spread flat between passes through the pleater, cut 20 pleating threads 24 inches (61 cm) long.

Tie the threads off in pairs at the very ends of the threads before pleating the next section.

1. Mark the fabric with a pressed fold to guide the pleating. Turn under 5 inches (12.5 cm) on one long edge and press a fold. Unfold it. The 5-inch (12.5-cm) area will be pleated horizontally for the ruffle at the top of the purse. The remaining 13-inch (33-cm) section will be pleated in vertical stripes.

2. With the fabric flat, press a fold 1 inch (2.5 cm) from one short edge of the fabric to serve as a guide for the first needle to follow as you pleat the first pass.

3. With the fold matching needle 1, start the fabric through the pleater until it can be seen on the needles; then thread the needles.

4. Starting with needle 1 (the farthest from the handle), thread two needles, leave three unthreaded, thread two, leave three until you reach the end of the pleater. Unless the fabric is very fragile, leave all needles in the pleater.

Designer: SARAH DOUGLAS

The unthreaded ones will give stability to the pleating.

On a 16-row pleater, thread the remaining needle of the pair at the handle end. When you have finished the first pass through the pleater, press a fold following that single thread and then remove the thread. The fold will guide needle 1 again. Finish the tenth stripe by hand with an uneven running stitch to match the pleater spacing.

On a 24-row pleater, leave the next-to-the top needle unthreaded, but thread the top needle. This thread will serve as a guide for the next pass through the pleater. Do not thread needles 1 and 2 on the next pass. Needle 1 will follow the thread from the last pass. Needle 2 is the third unthreaded needle. Needles 3 and 4 are the first stripe made in this pass. Remove the guide thread when you finish pleating the piece.

Pleating

1. After threading, pull the fabric over the eyes of the needles and turn the gear side toward you. Work until the horizontal foldline disappears into the gears.

2. Turn the pleater around, needle side toward you again. Take the removable gear out, and lift the fabric out carefully with all the needles in place. Pull the needles through the fabric, leaving the threads. Pull back the threads until there is 1/2 to 5/8 inch (1.5 cm) seam allowance at the bottom of the bag. At the top, pull the threads back until they all end at least one pleat below the horizontal fold. Working at the very ends of the threads, tie the threads in pairs. Spread the fabric out on the threads but don't press it.

3. Replace the needles and removable gear. Roll the fabric into a tube again and position it so that the next guide, a thread or a fold, matches needle 1. Repeat until the desired number of stripes are made (the model has ten).

4. Spread the fabric again and pleat the horizontal band at the top for the ruffle. Don't roll the fabric. With the needle side facing you, start the 5-inch (12.5-cm) section into the pleater at the not-handle end and let the rest of it lie on the table behind the pleater. Needle 1 will follow the fold. Use 28-inch (71-cm) threads to thread the needles that will go through the fabric. If there will be more than a half-space of fabric beyond the last needle at the cut edge, use a half-space needle there so the pleating threads will run as close to the cut edge as possible.

5. Feed the fabric into the gears a little at a time, keeping the inch or so directly behind the gears flat and moving evenly.

Keep the pleats packed tightly together on the threads as you work. When the pleating is finished, tie both ends of the threads in pairs and push all the pleats against one end as tightly as possible.

6. Steam the piece thoroughly to set the pleats, holding the iron so it just touches the fabric. Pull the pleats of the stripes up against the thread at the ruffle end and steam them just enough to make the peaks crisp and easy to pick up on a needle. Allow the piece to dry.

7. Spread the fabric and do the basic construction of the outer bag before smocking. Stitch two rows of gathering threads in the lower seam allowance without catching the pleating threads.

8. To seam the piece into a round, measure the distance between pairs of pleated stripes on the lower half and divide by two. This is the space between the last stripe on each end and the seamline. Mark it on the wrong side or press folds up to, but not through, the pleating of the top section.

9. Spread the pleats of the upper section and cut the knots off the ends of those pleating threads. Pull the threads back so they are inside the seam line. Tie them again at the ends. Trim the seam allowances to 1/2 inch (1.3 cm).

10. For the upper section, use a French seam (the body of the bag will be lined and the seam won't show). Pin the seam, wrong sides together, to the bottom of the ruffle. Match the pleating threads; the seam should join the valleys or the peaks of two pleats. Stitch 1/4 inch (.7 cm) from the edge. Trim and press, taking care not to flatten the pleats. Fold, with right sides together, along the stitching line, again matching the pleating threads. Stitch with 1/4 inch (.7 cm) seam allowance. Press.

Stitch the remainder of the seam with right sides together and press it open.

FINE CORDED PIPING DEFINES THE SEAMLINE AROUND THE BOTTOM OF THE BAG.

11. Finish the edge of the ruffle, or treat it to protect it during smocking. Machine stitch close to the edge, or apply fray retardant liberally along the edge (test it first on a scrap of fabric). The ruffle edge might also be stitched to give it a lettuce finish.

Smocking

Use a single strand of thread, or a double strand if the thread is very fine. Add beads as you stitch, as shown on the chart.

1. For the stripes on the body of the bag, work cable and half-space wave stitches as illustrated. Alternate the pattern sequence so that for the second and fourth stripes, etc., the cable stitch row is at the bottom rather than the top of the sequence. Pull out the pleating threads.

2. The smocking at the base of the ruffle (not visible in the photo) also creates a channel for the drawstring. Working upward from the pleated section, work one row of cable, incorporating beads as shown.

3. Between rows 2 and 3, work full-space wave. Then work another wave stitch row in the same space so the stitches overlap as in the illustration. Omit beads from this stitching.

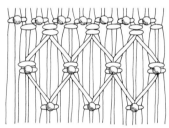

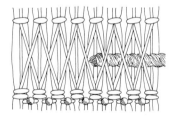

ABOVE: CABLE STITCH AND HALF-SPACE WAVES FOR STRIPES ON THE BAG BODY. BELOW: A DOUBLE ROW OF WAVE STITCH CREATES A CHANNEL FOR THE DRAW

Assembly

1. Stitch a gathering line 1/4 inch (.7 cm) from the edge of each fabric circle. Draw up a circle around a plastic piece, but do not tie off the thread. Steam the edges—

the pressed fold will be the seamline. Allow to dry, then loosen the gathering and remove the plastic.

2. Make piping. Wrap the fabric strip, right side out, around the cord. Stitch to the right side of the outer fabric circle along the marked seamline. Put the plastic back in and pull the gathering thread up to hold it.

3. Construct the lining. Stitch the two short ends of the rectangle, right sides together. Press. For the top, turn under one long edge 1/2 inch and stitch close to the fold with a gathering stitch. Stitch two gathering rows in the 1/2 inch (1.3 cm) seam allowance on the remaining long edge.

4. Gather the lower edges of the outer bag and lining to fit the lining circle seamline. The outside of the bag is longer than the lining. Keep the stripes flat and put the extra fullness in the puffy areas between them.

5. Place the lining in the bag with wrong sides together. Baste the two layers together around the bottom, matching the side seams. Stitch to the lining circle along the foldline (an open embroidery foot is helpful in sewing over the beads). Tuck the plastic back into the circle, pull up the gathering threads again and tie them off. Steam the seams toward the circle.

6. Slip stitch the piped circle to the bottom of the purse by hand.

7. With the neck of the bag stretched slightly, ease the lining edge to fit, the folded edge of the lining at the cable row. Slip stitch the lining in place, working into the backs of the pleats.

Finishing

1. Fold the purse with the seam as center back and, just above the smocking of the ruffle, make a small buttonhole on each side for the drawstring. As an alternative, soak the area with fray retardant, allow it to dry, then simply cut slits.

2. Cut the decorative cord in half. Feed one length out through a buttonhole, around the bag under the wave stitch, then out of the stitching to the inside through the same buttonhole. Knot the ends together. Work the other cord from the other side of the bag.

3. Decorate the turn-down of the ruffle by working chain stitch in random rows of uneven length on the peaks of the pleats. Add a few beads here and there and at the ends of the rows.

PENDANT POCKET PURSE

Designed to keep small valuables safe, this clever purse is popular around the world. An ornate outer pocket cover slides up the neck cord to reveal a secure inner pocket. It's a designer's dream, responding beautifully to any small-scale ornamentation: stitching, beading, fabric manipulation, or whatever decorative art you care to apply. It can be equally interesting made up of an especially pretty bit of purchased fabric with no further adornment at all.

This designer's specialty is machine embroidery. The rabbit and turnip motif on the carved jade pendant provided inspiration for the stitching. She painted small areas of the fabric with dye, then worked the design in free-motion straight stitch, with satin stitch for the bow on the inner pocket.

Free-motion stitching is great fun. If you've never tried it, read the tips on page 14.

Ornaments on both the pocket and pocket cover double as handles for easy opening and closing. On the inner pocket, sew a short strand of beads, a tassel, or a small pendant to the center of the lower edge. On the pocket cover, attach a handle at each lower corner. The tassels and the twisted cord on this model were made with the same thread that was used for the embroidery.

The finished size is 4-1/4 inches (10.75 cm) wide by 6 inches (15 cm) high. Made slightly larger, it could hold sunglasses or a passport as well as cash and credit cards.

Designer: **dj** BENNET

MATERIALS

Fabric: approximately 1/4 yard (.25 m) total for pocket cover, pocket, and pocket lining

Cord: 1 yard (1 m), approximately 3/8 inch (1 cm) diameter

Fusible interfacing: 1-1/2 by 24 inches (4 by 61 cm)

Decorative materials and objects: beads, buttons, tassels, special threads, fabric paints or dyes, whatever your design requires

INSTRUCTIONS

For machine embroidery, piecing, appliqué, or other decorative techniques that require a good bit of stitching, cut the pieces larger than the dimensions given and trim them to size after the stitching is finished. Seam allowances are 1/4 inch (.7 cm).

Cutting

1. For the pocket cover front and back, cut two pieces 4-3/4 inches (12.25 cm) wide and 7-3/4 inches (19.5 cm) long.

2. For the inner pocket and lining, cut four pieces 3-3/4 by 7-1/2 inches (9.5 by 19.5 cm).

Construction

1. With right sides together, stitch the pocket cover front and back along the long edges.

2. Stitch one end, beginning and ending 3/8 inch (1 cm) from the side seamlines.

3. Apply a strip of interfacing to the wrong side of the remaining edge. Clean finish the edge and press 1-1/2 inches (4 cm) to the wrong side. Stitch invisibly, or edgestitch and tack at the side seamlines. Turn right side out, and press.

4. Stitch channels for the cord 3/8 inch (1 cm) from each side. This stitching is not essential; omit it if it will interfere with your design.

5. Stitch "handles" securely at the lower ends of the outer seams.

6. Make the inner pocket. For the outer section, position the handle on the right side of the front lower edge, the attachment ends at the raw edge. Baste. Stitch the back and front along this edge and the two long edges with right sides together.

7. Fuse a strip of interfacing to the wrong side along the raw edge. Turn 1-1/2 inches (4 cm) to the wrong side; press.

8. Stitch the lining sections with right sides together on the long edges and one end. Apply interfacing and press the upper raw edge as above.

9. Thread the neck cord up through one channel in the pocket cover and down through the other so that the loop is at the top. Stitch about 1 inch (2.5 cm) of each cord end to the side seamline on the lining wrong side.

10. Slip the lining into the pocket. Match the upper edges and whipstitch or edgestitch them together.

A Bag from a Scarf

A beautiful handwoven scarf, particularly one made by someone special, deserves to be seen more often than it might when it is worn only as an accompaniment to your best winter coat. It's a quick matter to convert it into a pretty and practical bag, useful all year round.

The fabric of this scarf is very soft and rather loosely woven, so we lined it with firm cotton corduroy for stability. The fringe on this scarf provided the perfect place to display a collection of tiny charms and favorite beads and at the same time give added weight to the flap end to keep it in place.

Materials

Winter-weight scarf (or fabric yardage), 8-1/2 inches (21.5 cm) wide; 24 inches (61 cm) long excluding the fringe, 42 inches (107 cm) long with fringe

Lining fabric, 8-1/2 by 20 inches (21.5 by 50.5 cm)

Decorative cord for strap, 3/8 inch (1 cm) in diameter and approximately 48 inches (122 cm) long

Scrap of suede or synthetic suede, 2 inches (5 cm) square

Charms, buttons, or beads (we used approximately 100)

Designer: **Dee Dee Triplett**

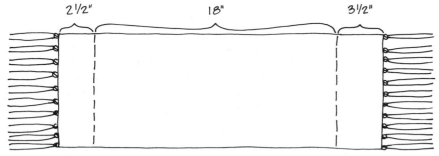

2½"   **18"**   **3½"**

POSITION THE LINING AS INDICATED BY THE DOTTED LINES.

INSTRUCTIONS

If you use fabric yardage instead of a scarf, clean finish or press under the long edges of the piece to the dimensions given above. Remove threads from the ends of the fabric to create the fringe, or clean-finish the ends and add purchased trim or fringe.

1. If desired, make a knotted fringe at each end of your scarf or fabric. Separate the long threads into an even number of small bundles. Beginning at one side, tie two bundles together in a square knot all the way across. Start the next row of knots on the same side, skip the first bundle and tie the second and third together, then the fourth and fifth together, and continue across. On the third row, begin again with the first and second bundles so the rows of knots are staggered. Add more rows of knots if you wish, until the result pleases your eye.

2. Press under 1 inch (2.5 cm) at each end of the lining fabric. Position the lining right side up on the wrong side of the fabric as shown in the diagram.

3. By hand or machine, stitch the lining to the outer fabric across the ends, stitching close to the folded edges of the lining. In loosely woven fabric, machine stitching will be nearly invisible.

4. Fold the bag right side out as shown, matching the lining ends. Stitch up each side as far as the ends of the lining using 1/4 inch (.7 cm) seam allowances. Trim away the lining seam allowances close to the stitching.

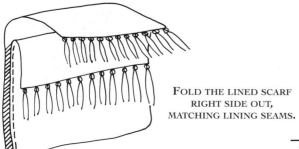

FOLD THE LINED SCARF
RIGHT SIDE OUT,
MATCHING LINING SEAMS.

5. Overcast the seam allowances with a zigzag or decorative overcast stitch, enclosing the lining raw edges inside these seams.

6. Add the strap. At the underside of the outer (longer) flap, abut the ends of the cord at the center of the lining edge. Trim one edge of the suede scrap to a pleasing shape, and position the opposite edge under the cord ends at the lining edge as shown.

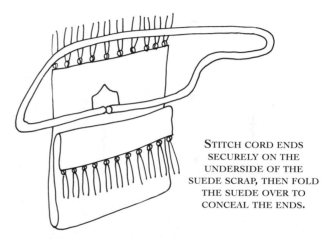

STITCH CORD ENDS
SECURELY ON THE
UNDERSIDE OF THE
SUEDE SCRAP, THEN FOLD
THE SUEDE OVER TO
CONCEAL THE ENDS.

7. Zigzag the cord ends firmly in place, securing the edge of the suede at the same time. Fold the trimmed end of the suede down over the cord. Stitch close to the edges of the piece and along the edge of the cord. With a permanent marker (we used gold metallic), personalize the bag with your initials.

8. Attach beads and charms to the fringe of the outer flap. Thread one or two of the fringe threads through each bead (a dental floss threader is a helpful tool for this task), staggering the placement. Knot the fringe securely below each bead to keep it in place.

Designer: NELL PAULK

A NEEDLEPOINT SAMPLER

This designer particularly likes working samplers. Before one pattern can become tedious, it's time to start the next.

An original piece of needle art deserves more attention than it gets as a pillow, hidden away in a corner of the couch, or framed and hung in a rarely used guest room. Convert it to a handbag and it will often be seen, gathering in the compliments it deserves.

Despite its rich appearance, this bag is a simple envelope, edged with a knitted garter stitch band and finished off with a custom-designed closure. The heavy silk lining (an appropriate fabric for such a work of art) has a wide pocket across the back. The finished bag is 10 inches (25.5 cm) wide and 6-1/2 inches (16.5 cm) high.

MATERIALS

Bargello canvas, 13 count, 10 by 17-1/2 inches (25.5 by 44.5 cm)

Lining fabric, the size of the canvas, plus additional for a pocket

Persian yarn in assorted colors

Beads or button, for the closure

INSTRUCTIONS

1. In planning the sampler, allow a margin of 1/2 inch (1.3 cm) at one short end of the canvas and 1/4 inch (.7 cm) on the other three sides.

2. Use the drawing as a guide, or make a sketch to plan a design. Begin with diagonal ribbon bands to work in basketweave, always a true diagonal. Then fill in with a variety of colors and patterns.

3. Turn under and steam press the 1/2-inch (1.3-cm) margin.

4. If a pocket will be added to the lining, mark across the fabric 5-1/2 inches (14 cm) from the top and 6 inches (15 cm) from the bottom. The center section will be at the bag back. Position the upper edge of the pocket below the upper marked line.

5. Fold the lower edge of the lining 1/2 inch (1.3 cm) to the wrong side; press.

6. Place the canvas and lining wrong sides together with the pressed edges aligned. Stitch together close to the edge, and again approximately 1/4 inch (.5 cm) away.

7. Place the piece lining side up, the finished edge at the bottom. Stitch together around the remaining three sides, approximately 1/4 inch (.7 cm) from the edges. Overcast.

8. Fold the lower edge up 6 inches (15 cm). Steam press, and allow to dry completely.

9. Meantime, knit a strip of garter stitch 1-1/2 inches (4 cm) wide and 33 inches (84 cm) long with one of the Persian yarn colors. Don't bind off; leave the stitches on a holder so length can be adjusted later.

10. Stitch the side seams of the bag, 1/4 inch (.7 cm) from the edges.

11. Beginning at one lower corner, fold the knitted band around the edge. With transparent thread, sew the edges of the band to the bag, up the side, across the flap, and down the other side. Adjust the band length if necessary, and bind off. Stitch the halves of the band together at the bottom of the bag.

12. For the button loop, knit a 12-inch (30-cm) length of I-cord. Loop it artistically, and stitch it to the flap.

13. Attach the bead with braided strands of yarn.

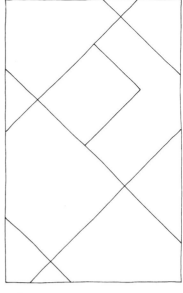

STITCHING DIAGRAM FOR THE NEEDLEPOINT SAMPLER.

T-Shirt Revised

Sweatshirts and T-shirts fairly call out for embellishment. It's fun to make a matching bag at the same time. Friends will think you've discovered a wonderful new boutique!

The designer began with a long-sleeved black tee with ribbed cuffs, and created a colorful shirt *and* a bag. She used a discharge technique to remove color, fabric paints to add new color, and some clever stitching to create the bag. If you start with a white or light-colored shirt, you can simply paint the designs you like or draw them with fabric marking pens.

Designer: PEGGY DEBELL

MATERIALS

T-shirt, cotton or cotton/polyester, with long sleeves and cuffs. Buy it extra-large!

Small paint roller

Paint brushes

Household bleach

White vinegar

Fabric paints

Optional:

Rotary cutter and mat

INSTRUCTIONS

Removing color by the discharge method is unpredictable. With black especially, the color revealed by the bleaching may not be white or gray, but red, brown, or almost anything. Be prepared for surprises—they are half the fun.

Decorating the shirt

1. Machine wash and dry the shirt to remove chemical finishes that could interfere with coloring.

2. Prepare a solution of half bleach and half hot water for the discharge. In a clean bucket, mix a bottle of white vinegar with warm water.

3. On a protected surface, spread the shirt out smoothly. Place pieces of cardboard inside to keep bleach solution from soaking through.

4. Dip the paint roller into bleach solution, shake off the excess, and "paint" stripes on the shirt to remove color. Use a paintbrush for smaller areas. Work quickly, then flip the shirt over to repeat the design on the other side.

5. When you see results of the bleaching, put the shirt into the vinegar solution to stop the bleaching action. Stir it around, and let it soak for 10 minutes or so.

6. Launder and dry the shirt again.

7. Decorate the shirt with paints or marking pens. Follow the manufacturer's instructions for setting the paint.

Making the bag

1. Smooth out the shirt, on a cutting mat if possible. Arrange the sleeves so the folds are on the straight grain of the fabric. Chalk mark a line across each sleeve, 8 inches (20 cm) above the lower edge and perpendicular to the fold, and cut off the sleeves along the lines.

2. Cut off the hemmed lower edge in the same way. If the shirt has ribbing at the bottom, cut it off, then cut a strip approximately 1-1/2 inches (4 cm) wide from the lower edge.

3. Use the strip from the lower edge to make the bag strap. Fold under the raw edges, press, and topstitch.

4. Cut each sleeve open along the original seam, and trim away the stitching.

5. Flatten out the pieces and pin them with right sides together. Stitch the bag sides and bottom, keeping the cuffs at the opening of the bag.

6. Stitch the strap ends to the inside of the bag along the seams.

7. If desired, add a decorative button at the cuff area of the bag, and work a chain stitch loop through the opposite edge to button it.

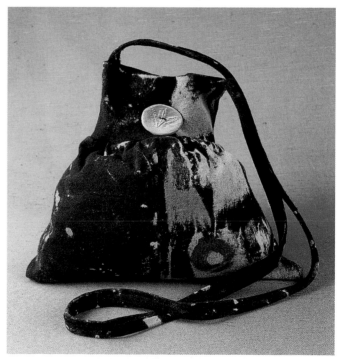

THIS VARIATION OF THE T-SHIRT BAG WAS PAINTED WITH A DIFFERENT DESIGN.

A Trilogy of Bags to Decorate

While many handbag designs respond to a little embellishment, this one is tailor-made for the purpose. The bag itself is quick and easy to assemble so you can spend your time at decorating the bag just as you'd like it to be. The three variations shown here are made of unbleached cotton muslin, a fabric that's inexpensive, easy to work with, and that makes a good background for all sorts of ornamentation.

This designer especially enjoys hand embroidery, and has incorporated a variety of stitches and decorative threads into her designs. Machine embroidery, tucks and pleats, appliqué, painting and stenciling—almost any decorative technique will work with this bag. Add a contrasting lining or edge binding and an exceptional button for a striking effect. Add a few tassels, making them as simple or as ornate as you wish. Experiment with a variety of materials for the strap, too: a single pretty ribbon, or twisted cord made up of colorful strands of embroidery floss, or an interesting purchased chain.

The construction of the bag can be varied, too. It can be made with a flap or with a zippered opening across the top. It can be sewn with bound seams on the right side, or in the conventional manner with piping along the seamline. Pockets can be added to the lining. The finished bag is 10-1/4 inches (26 cm) wide and 10-1/2 inches (26.5 cm) long.

MATERIALS

Fabric: 3/4 yard (.7 m) of 45-inch (115-cm) fabric is enough for the outer bag, lining, and edge binding

Garment-weight batting: 1/2 yard (.5 m)

Button or snap closure for bag with flap

Cord, chain, or fabric for strap

Materials for decorating, according to your design

INSTRUCTIONS

If the bag will be decorated, cut the outer fabric sections and batting larger than the pattern. Indicate the seamlines to guide your design. Add the embellishment, then trim the piece to size.

Bag with a Flap

Seam allowance of 3/8 inch (1 cm) is included on the pattern.

1. Enlarge the pattern (page 104) and cut from paper.

2. Cut one back/flap, one back/flap lining, and one back/flap batting from the pattern.

3. Cut one front, one front lining, and one front batting to the line indicated on the pattern.

4. For edge binding, cut bias strips 2 inches (5 cm) wide. Piece them as necessary for a total length of 1 3/4 yards (1.6 m).

5. Decorate the outer bag sections according to your design. If the embellishment plan includes a good bit of surface stitching, first baste the batting to the outer fabric to provide support for the stitching.

6. Add a pocket to the back lining section, if you wish.

7. With wrong sides together, baste the outer fabric and lining sections together, sandwiching the batting between. Trim outer fabrics to the lining pieces.

8. Bind the upper (straight) edge of the bag front section. With right sides together, sew a strip along the edge. Turn and press. On the lining side, fold under the raw edge so the fold just covers the previous stitching. On the right side, stitch in the ditch created by the first stitching line, catching the folded edge.

9. Stitch the front to the back with lining sides together, matching the lower points. Trim.

10. Bind the outer edges as for the bag front. Clip at the corners to miter them neatly, and fold under the overlapping end of the binding. On the lining side, the binding can be hand stitched in place if this works better with your fabric.

11. Use a 4-inch (10-cm) length of bias to make a button loop. Press in half, lengthwise, right side out, and press the ends under. Fold the raw edges in to the center crease; press. Edgestitch all sides. Fold in half, overlapping the ends, and sew onto the bag flap.

12. Sew the button at the bag front.

13. Knot the ends of the strap and stitch securely in place at the upper edges of the bag back binding.

Zippered bag without flap

In addition to the materials listed on the preceding page, you will need a 9-inch (23-cm) zipper. If the decoration for the bag involves heavy stitching, cut the outer fabric and batting larger, then trim them to size after the stitching is finished.

1. Use the bag front cutting line on the pattern to cut all pieces. Cut two pieces of batting to that line. For the outer bag and lining, add 3/8 inch (1 cm) seam allowance above the marked upper line of the pattern. Cut two pieces from outer fabric and two from lining by the revised pattern.

2. Decorate the outer bag sections according to your design. If the design includes much surface stitching, first baste the batting to the outer fabric to stabilize the fabric. When the stitching is complete, trim the pieces to the size of the lining pieces. Trim the batting close to the seamlines.

3. Install the zipper. Place the zipper and one outer bag section with right sides together, aligning the bag and zipper seamlines. Stitch; press the seam allowances toward the bag. Repeat for the other zipper edge.

4. Baste the batting to the wrong side of each bag section if this has not been done.

5. With right sides together, sew the bag front and back sections along the sides and lower edges. Trim the batting close to the stitching.

6. If desired, add a pocket to one or both lining sections.

Designer: **PEG MORRIS**

7. Stitch the lining front and back, right sides together, along the sides and lower edges, ending the stitching 3/4 inch (2 cm) from the upper edge at each side. Trim; press.

8. Press under 3/4 inch (2 cm) at the lining upper edges.

9. Place the lining in the bag. Whipstitch the lining to the zipper tape around the opening.

10. Knot the strap ends and stitch securely to the upper ends of the side seams.

STENCILED LEAVES

Off-white cotton makes a perfect backdrop for autumn-colored leaves. Narrow ribbons are couched by hand with pearl cotton, and narrow decorative braids add interesting texture and angles. The tassel is made of pearl cotton, trimmed with floss to match the leaf colors. The strap, too, is pearl cotton, twisted into a cord that is both pretty and sturdy. The lining and edge trim are lighter weight cotton fabric.

MATERIALS
In addition to the materials listed on page 100, you will need:

Acetate: a small piece, for the stencil

Sharp craft knife

fabric paints

Small sponge

Assorted ribbons and trims for embellishment

Pearl cotton, one skein

INSTRUCTIONS
1. Wash, dry, and press the fabric to be stenciled.

2. Cut the fabrics according to the instructions for the bag with a flap.

3. Enlarge the stencil pattern, trace it onto the acetate, and cut out the design.

4. Pour a small amount of fabric paint into a saucer for the stenciling. Dip the sponge lightly, and apply it to the fabric from the center outward. Allow the paint to dry, then set it according to the instructions with the paint.

5. Baste the batting to the wrong side of the stenciled fabrics, then add the couched ribbons and decorative trim.

6. Assemble the bag following the basic instructions.

PAISLEY PASTELS (shown on page 104)
Get out your favorite book of embroidery stitches to embellish this design. With the appliqué pattern as a guide, add lacy stitches, satin stitch borders, and French knots. Top it off with small pieces of contrasting fabric, applied with metallic thread, and a few seed beads for good measure.

Pastel striped cotton was used for the outer bag, with embroidery threads and applied fabrics in colors to match the stripes. For the strap and tassels (tassel instructions are on page 6), pearl cotton works beautifully. The strap is a twisted cord (page 6), knotted at the ends and stitched to the side seamlines.

The lower corners of the bag were rounded slightly for smoother insertion of the narrow corded piping. It has a zippered opening across the top. The lining, shown on page 5, includes a long, divided pocket to keep small items organized.

APPLIQUÉ MOTIFS, LEAF AND PAISLEY DESIGNS. ENLARGE 222%.

Designer: PEG MORRIS

TUCKS AND BEADS

Two complementary fabrics—one plain and one patterned—are tucked and stitched, then cut and rearranged to create an altogether new fabric. As you can see, this is a design scheme with plenty of potential. The bag's interior is like a star-studded evening sky with an unexpected lining of synthetic suede and a sprinkling of bugle beads.

INSTRUCTIONS

The bag is made according to the instructions for the bag with a flap. Cut the batting and lining first, and use the lining as a guide for shape and size of the patchwork.

1. For the outer bag piecing, choose a pleasing combination of fabrics and cut several rectangles the size of the bag front, or wider.

2. With one of the rectangles, begin approximately 1 inch (2.5 cm) from a short side and fold the fabric, right sides together, along the fabric grain. Press the crease, then stitch approximately 3/8 inch (1 cm) from the fold. Make another fold parallel with the first; press and stitch it as before. Work your way across the fabric this way, spacing the tucks evenly or unevenly, as you prefer, but always making them along the grain. Stitch several more rectangles in the same way.

3. Now for the fun! Cut the tucked pieces into strips (remember you will need seam allowance at each cut edge). Make the cuts perpendicular to the stitched tucks, or on the diagonal.

4. Assemble the cut pieces in any sort of order. Stitch two together along the cut edges, then add another, and so on. Make a piece for the front and one for the back of the bag.

5. Trim the pieces to the lining, and baste the batting in place.

6. Add any other ornamentation you'd like. On the model, bugle beads are stitched to two of the tucked sections. A narrow ribbon is shaped, then stitched in place with French knots; another is couched with hand stitches.

7. Add beads to the lining, too, if desired.

8. Finish the assembly and bind the edges of the bag.

9. Add a tassel made of pearl cotton to match the lining (see page 6). For the strap, an inexpensive purchased necklace serves very well.

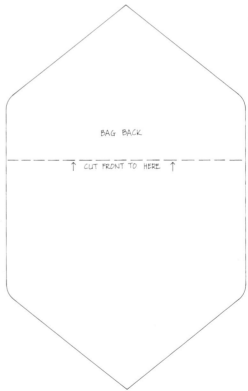

BAG BACK

↑ CUT FRONT TO HERE ↑

PATTERN, BAG FRONT AND BACK/FLAP.
ENLARGE 400%. CUT BAG BACK/FLAP
AND LINING FROM THE FULL PATTERN;
CUT FRONTS AS INDICATED.

Designer: PEG MORRIS

TASSELED BAG

Tassels—a baker's dozen of them—transform a merely gorgeous bag into one that's quite remarkable. The colorful bargello pattern is a treat to stitch. It goes along quickly, with frequent color changes to keep things interesting. Across the top and bottom are bands of basketweave stitch for contrast.

And as for the tassels, use a different yarn color for each one, then wrap and decorate every one in a different way. Add a few French knots and an embroidery stitch or two. Once you get started, you'll find it difficult to stop! Basic tasselmaking instructions are on page 6.

The bag zips across the top, with a tassel as the zipper pull. The wrist strap is braided strands of yarn, finished, of course, with tassels. The bag is 10 inches (25.5 cm) wide and 8 inches (20 cm) high.

Designer: NELL PAULK

MATERIALS

Bargello canvas, 13 count, 11 by 17 inches (28 by 43 cm)

Lining fabric, 11 by 17-3/4 inches (28 by 45 cm) plus additional for a pocket

Persian yarn in assorted colors

Zipper, 9-inch (23-cm) length

INSTRUCTIONS

Seam allowances are 1/2 inch (1.3 cm) except as noted.

1. Plan the stitch pattern, following the diagram or your own design. Allow 1/2 inch (1.3 cm) margin on all sides of the canvas. Mark a line across the piece at the center, and plan the 1-inch (2.5-cm) basketweave strip here. Work a similar basketweave strip at each end. Work the stitching.

2. Fold the piece in half crosswise, right sides together, and stitch the side seams. Steam press. Fold under the margin at the opening; press. Allow the piece to dry.

3. Make the lining. Add a pocket, if desired, in the back section, placing the upper edge approximately 2 inches (5 cm) below the upper edge of the lining.

4. Install the zipper. Stitch to one short edge of the lining, right sides together, matching seamlines. Stitch

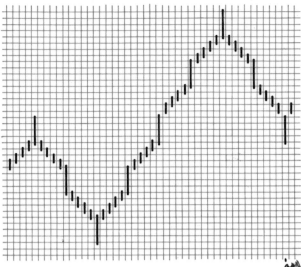

BARGELLO PATTERN FOR THE TASSELED BAG.

the other end of the lining to the other side of the zipper in the same way.

5. Fold the lining, wrong sides together, with the zipper at the top. Stitch the sides with French seams, incorporating the ends of the zipper tape in the second lines of stitching.

6. So the zipper will be recessed at the top of the bag, on the lining right side, press a pleat all around the zipper, the crease 3/8 inch (1 cm) from the zipper seamline.

7. Put the lining into the bag, zipper open. Pin the folded edge of the lining just below the bag edge. Stitch the lining to the bag, stitching close to the lining fold, then again just above the zipper seamline.

8. Make the tassels—as many as you'd like.

9. For the wrist strap, braid a total of nine strands of yarn to a length of 15 inches (38 cm). Incorporate three tassels into each end of the braid. Sew one end securely to an upper front corner, the other to the back.

10. Sew the remaining tassels down the side of the bag opposite the wrist strap.

CHAPTER 7

BAGS AS JEWELRY

Very small bags are a wonderful jewelry alternative. They are inexpensive, they can be every bit as colorful and glitzy and decorative as any necklace, and they are great fun to design and make. Because of the diminutive size, it is easy to put together one or two in an evening. And yours will be absolutely unique.

CROCHET WITH GEMSTONES

The flap of this small crocheted bag provides a wonderful setting for a handful of tiny gems or a collection of intriguing beads. The bag is sized to hold a credit card and keys, and perhaps an important message or two. It's quick to crochet—with a border of birthstones, it's a thoughtful birthday gift for a deserving person.

The model bag is edged with pre-drilled lapis chips and crocheted in a slubbed cotton yarn. It is 4-1/4 inches (10.5 cm) wide, 4-1/2 inches (11.5 cm) long.

Designer: AMY MOZINGO

MATERIALS

Yarn: 3-ply, or a combination of threads equal to that thickness, approximately 1-3/4 ounces (50g)

Crochet hook: U.S. size E

Stone chips or beads

Strong craft thread

Needle: a size that will go through the holes in the stones

INSTRUCTIONS

Crochet abbreviations are explained on page 59.

A long rectangle forms the front, back and flap. The edge of the flap is shaped. A side gusset continues to form the strap.

Gauge: sc, ch 1, sc, ch 1, sc equals 5/8 inch (1.5 cm); 4 rows equal 1/2 inch (1.3 cm).

Row 1: Chain 29. Sc in 4th ch from hook. Ch 1, skip 1 chain stitch, sc to end of chain (13 sc plus first ch 3). Ch 3, turn.

Row 2: Sc in ch 1 space of previous row, (ch 1, sc in next space). Repeat to end of row.

Repeat row 2 until piece is approximately 12-1/2 inches (32 cm) long.

Shaped flap edge

For the shaped rows at the flap edge, one scallop will be worked at a time. First scallop:

Row 1: Work in pattern for 11 sc. Ch 1, turn.

Row 2: Work in pattern to end of row. Ch 3, turn.

Row 3: Work in pattern to end of row. Ch 1, turn.

Repeat rows 2 and 3 until only about 3 or 4 sc remain in the row. Fasten off and weave the ends into the previous stitches to finish.

Second scallop:

Row 1: Attach yarn in ch 1 space next to the last sc in flap Row 1. Ch 1, sc to end of row, ch 3, turn.

Row 2: Crochet in pattern to end of row. Ch 1, turn.

Row 3: Crochet in pattern to end of the row. Ch 3, turn.

Repeat rows 2 and 3 until only 2 or 3 sc remain in the row. Fasten off and weave the ends into the previous stitches to finish.

Add the stones

With strong thread to match, sew the stone chips or beads to the irregular edge just formed on the flap. Take care not to add too many; the weight can affect the way the flap will hang.

Side gussets and strap

Row 1: Ch 8, sc in 4th ch from hook. Sc, ch 1, skip 1 ch, sc. Ch 3, turn.

Row 2 and on: Crochet in pattern to a length of approximately 42 inches (107 cm).

Finishing

Fold the purse section in half (exclude the flap) and pin the gusset/strap piece to the purse front area, taking care to line up the ch 3 spaces on the sides. Pin an end of the gusset at the bottom of the purse body to form the lower corners, so that the body of the purse forms a U around the gusset.

Crochet or sew the gusset in place. Start at the top of the purse front; work around the bottom and up the back. Attach the back only to the point on the gusset where the front is attached; the remainder of the piece is the flap. Repeat for the other side, taking care not to twist the strap.

MACHINE EMBROIDERY

Larger versions of these charming purses are shown in the preceding chapters; scaled down in size they are just as attractive and every bit as much fun to make. Very small scraps that you have hoarded can be displayed very nicely this way.

Free-motion quilting gives the bags their personality. Wonderfully diverse effects can be created by using different threads and different stitching patterns, and by strategic application of other fabrics. Detailed instructions for the technique are on page 14.

When the bag is very small, the closure becomes a more prominent feature and can be the focal point of the whole design. On the blue bag, handmade glass beads inspired the design. A larger teardrop-shaped one serves as a button, with several smaller ones to anchor the button loop to the flap. An appropriate wooden toggle buttons the bag worked in autumn colors, a nice complement to the color scheme.

MATERIALS

Both bags are simply rectangles, folded up from the bottom, then folded down from the top to form the flap. The bags illustrated are 4 inches (10 cm) and 6 inches (15 cm) square when closed, but any size will work. Cut fabric sizes slightly larger all around than you will need, work the stitching, then trim to the size you will need. Add narrow seam allowances only on the sides. You will need:

> Fabric for the outer bag
>
> Lining fabric
>
> Garment-weight batting or cotton flannel: the size of the outer fabric piece
>
> Fabric for edge binding, button loop, and strap: to match or complement the outer bag fabric
>
> An interesting closure

CONSTRUCTION

Remember to cut fabrics slightly larger than needed because dense stitching will draw them up slightly.

Stitching the layers

1. Layer the fabric rectangles, the outer fabric and lining right side out with the batting between. Pin baste.

Designer: **KAREN SWING**

2. To stabilize the fabric for stitching, spray starch one side of the piece, allow it to dry, then starch the other side.

3. Using the free-motion stitching technique, stitch over the entire piece to hold the layers together.

4. When the stitching is finished, trim the piece to the size needed.

Assembly

1. With right sides together, fold the lower edge of the bag upward and stitch the sides. Overcast the seam allowances neatly.

2. Shape the lower corners, if desired, to give the bag depth. With the bag wrong side out, fold each lower corner to create a point at the lower end of the seam. Stitch across the point approximately 1 inch (2.5 cm) from the end of the seam, stitching exactly perpendicular to the seamline as shown in the drawing on page 9.

3. Trim the sides of the flap so they are slightly narrower than the finished front of the bag (see the illustration on page 11). Round the corners slightly at the upper edges of the opening. Round the corners of the flap.

4. Serge or overcast all raw edges.

Edge binding and finishing

1. For the edge binding, cut a strip 1-1/2 inches (4 cm) wide and approximately 24 inches (61 cm) long. For smooth application, cut it on the bias.

2. Cut the strap on the lengthwise fabric grain, 1-1/2 inches (4 cm) wide and 43 inches (109 cm) long, or the desired length.

3. Cut a button strip 1-1/2 inches (4 cm) wide and to the length desired. It can be sewn into the flap edge binding as shown on the rust and gold bag, or it can be attached creatively to the outer flap as on the blue bag.

4. For the strap, sew the long edges of the strip, right sides together, using 1/4 inch (.7 cm) seam allowance. Turn and press. Alternatively, press the strip in half, right side out. Fold the raw edges in to the center; press. Stitch along both long edges.

5. On the bag right side, align the strap ends with the edge of the bag at the side seamlines. Pin the button strip at the center front of the flap.

6. Beginning on the front, stitch the binding strip to the bag, right sides together and edges aligned, using 3/8 inch (1 cm) seam allowance. At the flap/front corners, ease the fabric and clip into the seam allowances as necessary. Fold under the overlapping end. Press binding toward the seam allowances.

7. Fold under the raw edge of the strip so the fold just covers the previous stitching line, and stitch by hand.

8. Sew the button on the bag front. If a shank button is not used, make a long thread shank for the button to accommodate the thickness of the button loop.

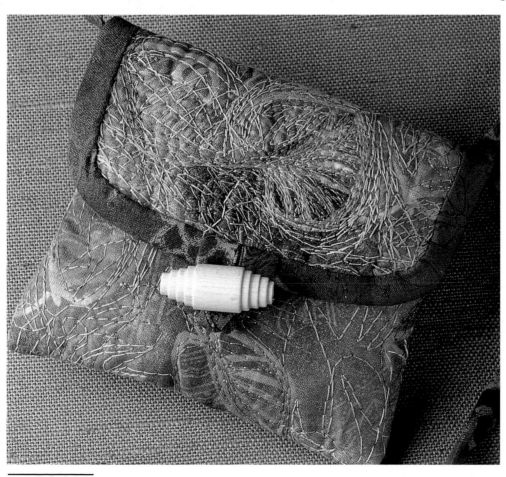

Designer: KAREN SWING

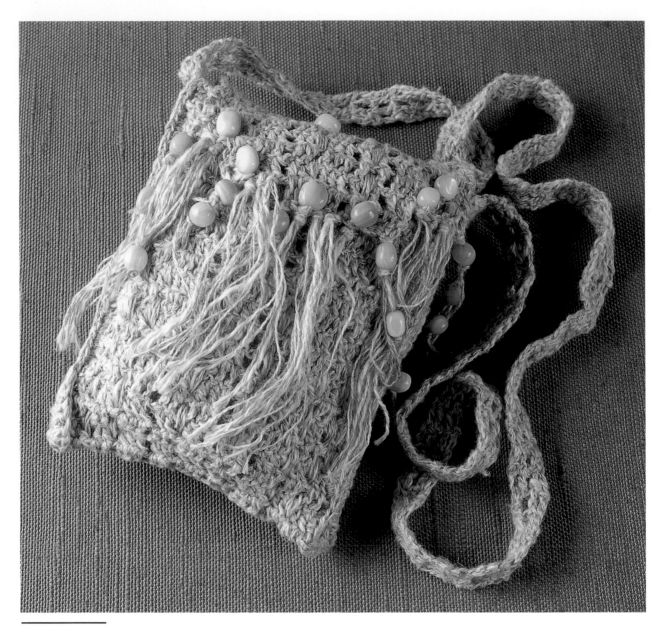

Designer: AMY MOZINGO

BEADS AND FRINGE

Lustrous moonstones are threaded onto the fringe along the flap of this small bag. The effect is more than just decorative—the additional weight keeps the flap closed and helps the bag hang attractively. Choose beads or gemstones with fairly large holes so that four strands of your chosen thread will pass through easily.

MATERIALS

Yarn: 3-ply yarn, or a combination of threads equal to that thickness, approximately 1-3/4 ounces (50g)

Crochet hook: U.S. size D

Moonstones, or other beads

INSTRUCTIONS

Crochet abbreviations are explained on page 59.

The finished bag is approximately 4-1/4 inches (10.5 cm) wide and 4-1/2 inches (11.5 cm) long. Gauge: 8 dc equal 1 inch (2.5 cm); 4 rows equal 1 inch (2.5 cm).

Chain 32.

Row 1: Ch 3 (counts as 1 dc), dc in 4th ch from hook, dc, ch 1, skip next base ch; 2 dc, ch, 3 dc, ch 2, 2 dc, ch, 3 dc, ch, dc, ch, dc, ch, 3 dc, ch, 2 dc, ch, 3 dc.

Rows 2 through row 44: Ch 3, turn. Follow pattern established in Row 1; dc in previous dc, ch over previous ch space.

Row 45: Ch 3, turn. Follow pattern until last ch space, ch 3 and turn. No stitches are made into the last 3 dc of the previous row.

Row 46: Follow pattern until last ch, 3 dc, ch, 3 dc. Ch 3 and turn. Again, skip the last 3 sts.

Row 47: Follow pattern until last ch, 3 dc, ch, 2 dc. End off.

Note: You can choose to crochet through row 47 as you did for the first 44 rows. The flap of the purse will have a straight edge.

Gusset/strap

The strap ends form gussets at the sides of the purse.

Row 1: Ch 8, dc in 4th ch from hook, ch 1 (skip 1 ch in base chain), 2 dc.

Row 2: Ch 3 (counts as 1st dc), dc, ch 1, 2 dc.

Row 3 and remaining rows: Continue in pattern until strap is approximately 42 inches (107 cm) long.

Decoration

It is easiest to add the beads before you sew the strap in place.

Treating four strands of thread as one, cut three pieces each 1 yard (1 m) long. These strands will be woven through the ch 1 spaces.

So that the purse will hang properly, place more of the beads toward the center of the flap; fewer at the sides.

Strand 1: Beginning at the irregular edge, weave the strand in and out of the ch 1 spaces. In the first weave or so, go through a bead as you weave. When you reach the end of the crocheted rectangle, wrap yarn around the end and continue weaving in the next row of ch 1 spaces. When back near the beginning, remember to weave through a bead.

Strand 2: Skip the next row of ch 1 spaces, weave as before but when you reach the end where you turn to weave back to the beginning, skip a ch 1 row and weave through the next ch 1 row. End as before.

Strand 3: Skip next ch 1 row and weave in the last two available rows.

Add fringe to the irregular edge, if you wish. Work doubled strands of thread through the last row of stitches, incorporating a bead here and there. Include the weaving ends in the fringe; this will knot the ends and keep the strands in place.

Assemble the purse

Fold the purse rectangle in half, excluding the flap portion, and mark the bottom. Pin the gusset/strap in place between the front and back, centering one end at the marked bottom of the bag. Pin along the sides.

Line up the rows across the gusset, and leave the front flap free. When you pin the second side, be sure the strap is not twisted. Work sc to join the pieces, beginning at one upper edge. Watch that the stitches don't ripple (too many) or pucker (too few) the purse. Usually, 2 sc in each dc will produce a smooth seam. At the corners, work 1 sc in the space, ch 1, 1 sc in same space.

At the upper edge, sc across the base ch at the top of the purse. Be sure to crochet around the woven strands wrapped around the chain. This helps secure the woven strands and neatens the top.

STITCHERY EXTRAVAGANZA

Very small bags offer a perfect medium for experimentation with new stitching techniques. At this size, even a complicated design takes little time. And if the results are far too bizarre to incorporate into a large-scale item or a garment, they should be very effective for a little purse.

This clever two-piece bag offers secure storage for small items. The outer pocket cover slides up the cords to reveal an inner pocket with a top opening. Each pocket offers a front and back for adornment—a chance to try four new techniques in one place. Complete instructions for making the bags begin on page 92.

Designer: **dj** BENNETT

PIECING IN MINIATURE

The pieced bag opposite shows just how effective the simplest patchwork can be. Strips of richly colored calicos make up the outer pocket. The inner pocket is a solid color, with calico prairie points stitched into the seam at the lower edge.

To make a prairie point, cut a fabric square. Fold it in half across so that the fold is at the top of the piece. Then fold each upper corner downward to the center of the lower edge as shown. Stitch the raw edges into the seam allowance.

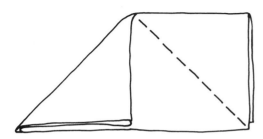

SMOCKING AND NEEDLE LACE

Both techniques are very traditional; the results are anything but! For the pocket cover, a central panel of linen fabric was pleated up, then smocked with just a few simple rows of stitches accented with beads.

For a small project like this, the fabric can be prepared without a smocking pleater. Define the area to be pleated with a chalk line at each side. Chalk-mark lines approximately 1/2 inch (1.3 cm) apart across the panel. Machine baste along each line, starting precisely on the vertical line each time so the stitches will be aligned vertically. Draw up the pleats and knot the threads together in pairs. Then work several rows of your favorite smocking stitches.

The inner pocket began with an openweave fabric in the same color. The fabric was slashed here and there, then restitched, with beads and Dorset wheel buttons added for good measure. The pocket front section extends beyond the bottom of the pocket (the lining is the standard size), providing a handy pull tab as well as a glimpse of the interior design.

To work this kind of needle lace, use a loose openweave fabric fairly light in weight. Tighten it into a hoop with a piece of water-soluble backing underneath. Cut slashes in the fabric, taking care not to cut the backing. Using the free-motion satin stitch technique described on page 14, stitch around the openings, bundling up some of the cut threads in the stitching.

Designer: **dj BENNETT**

CROCHETED MINIATURES

With a small amount of leftover yarn and a good video, you can crochet one of these charming bags in an evening. Each is slightly more than 2 inches (5 cm) in length, sized to carry a lucky charm or a little cash for emergencies.

Young girls love to wear the tiny purses. For older "girls," they make clever packaging for special small gifts.

Any fine yarn can be used for this project. If you run out of one color, just start with another. Or make the cord and tassels with a contrasting color. Even sewing thread will work—try four to six strands, perhaps blending the colors. Cotton embroidery floss is especially pretty; working with all six strands, it takes approximately three skeins to complete a bag.

Designer: AMY MOZINGO

SUNNY YELLOW BAG

Two very fine strands of nubby thread—a lighter and a darker shade—were used for the bag illustrated. It is crocheted in a spiral pattern from the bottom upward.

MATERIALS

Thread: fine 3-ply yarn, or a combination of threads of similar thickness

Crochet hook: U.S. size E

INSTRUCTIONS

Crochet abbreviations are explained on page 59.

Gauge: sc, ch 1, sc, ch 1, sc equals 5/8 inch (1.5 cm); 4 rows equal 1/2 inch (1.3 cm)

Row 1: Crochet a 4-stitch chain; join to form a loop. Ch 2, (sc, ch 1) in loop until beginning ch 2 stitch is reached (usually about 6 sc/ch 1 sets). Ch1, sc in the ch 2 stitch. The rows will now spiral up the bag.

Row 2: 2 (ch 1, sc) in first space formed by the ch 1 on the previous row. Ch 1, sc in next space. Repeat until back at beginning with a "double" stitch in every other space. Ch 1, sc in bridging stitch at the end of the last row.

Row 3: 2 (ch 1, sc) in the first space (between a double stitch on the previous row) ch 1, sc in the next 2 ch 1 spaces. Repeat until back at the beginning.

Remaining rows: Ch 1, sc in every ch 1 space until desired length of bag is reached, usually about 2 inches. Slip stitch into top of ch 1 space.

Neck cord row: Ch 4, dc in ch 1 space, ch 1, dc until last ch 1 space is filled. Fasten off and weave end into previous stitches.

Neck cord

Treating two thicknesses of thread as one, chain two lengths, each about 3 inches (7.5 cm) longer than the desired length of the neck cord. Weave the cords in and out of the dc stitches in the last row.

Tassel

Cut about four strands of thread (more for a thicker tassel) twice as long as the desired length of the tassel. Fold in half, and pull the loop formed through the end of a neck cord, pull the ends through the loop. Tighten by gently pulling all the threads evenly. Repeat on all four ends of the neck cords. Consider making a tassel for the bottom of the bag, too.

ECRU MINIATURE

It is made like the yellow bag, but the shape is slightly different. Our model was crocheted with two strands of a very fine two-ply yarn, a blend of silk, rayon, and cotton.

MATERIALS

Thread: fine 2-ply yarn, or thread to obtain gauge

Crochet hook: U.S. size D

INSTRUCTIONS

Crochet abbreviations are explained on page 59.

Gauge: Sc, ch 1, sc, ch 1, sc equals 5/8 inch (1.5 cm); 4 rows equal 1/2 inch (1.3 cm)

Row 1: Chain 15. Sc in 3rd chain from hook. (Ch 1, skip 1 chain, sc) to end of the chain. 2 (ch 1, sc) in the same last stitch to turn corner. Ch 1, sc over the chain on the other side, working the sc sts in the chain that was left open. When you reach the starting point, place an extra (ch 1, sc) in the last stitch to turn the corner; ch 1 and work 1 sc in the ch space made in the beginning. The rows will now spiral up the bag.

Row 2: (Ch 1, sc) working each sc in the ch 1 spaces of the previous row until the bag is approximately 2-1/4 inches (5.5 cm) long.

Neck cord row: Ch 4, dc in ch 1 space, ch 1, dc until last ch 1 space is filled. Fasten off and weave end into previous stitches.

Neck cord

Treating two thicknesses of yarn as one, chain two lengths, each about 3 inches (7.5 cm) longer than the desired length of the neck cord. Weave the cords in and out the dc stitches in the last row.

Tassel

Cut about four strands of thread (more for a thicker tassel) twice as long as the desired length of the tassel. Fold in half, pull the loop formed through the end of a neck cord, and pull the ends through the loop. Tighten by gently pulling all the threads evenly. Repeat on all four ends of the neck cords.

If you wish, tassels can be added to the lower corners of the bag, too.

CHAPTER 8

WHIMSICAL BAGS

The little bags in this chapter are not meant to be taken seriously—or are they? Despite the fact these designs are lighthearted in spirit, they may just get you thinking about purses in a new way. Make a quick inventory of the wealth of materials around you, then think about using some unorthodox materials or unconventional combinations in your own original design.

The Silly Answer

The question might be, "Just how far can you push a smocking pleater?" Or, "Is there anything new for a smocker to try?" For devotees of smocking, this miniature drawstring bag can serve as a unique package for a small gift. It could as easily be made full size, a decidedly out-of-the-ordinary handbag.

The "bag" is plastic screenwire, the kind sold in window screen repair kits. The stitching is worked with several strands of silk floss. Inside, a lining of silk keeps the contents hidden from view.

Designer: **Sarah Douglas**

Materials and Tools

Plastic screening, 4-1/2 by 24 inches
(11.5 by 61 cm)

Silk floss, or cotton floss, or heavy pearl cotton

Smocking pleater

Silk, for the lining, approximately 1/8 yard (.15 m)

Instructions

In order for the embroidery stitches to show up, use heavier thread or more strands of floss than you would use for fabric.

1. Cut a rectangle from the screening, 4-1/2 by 20 inches (11.5 by 50.5 cm), cutting carefully with the "grain" of the wire. Cut a circle 3-1/2 inches (9 cm) in diameter for the bottom of the bag. Mark 1/2 inch (1.3 cm) seam allowance around the perimeter of the circle.

2. Pleat five rows on the rectangle, the first one 1/2 inch (1.3 cm) from one long edge; this is the bottom.

3. Draw up the threads, shaping the bag. Fit the bottom to the circle seamline. Turn the seam allowances on both pieces to the inside, so that the seamline on the circle is fitted to the first pleating row. At the ends of the rectangle, turn the edge to the inside, overlapping them by approximately 1/4 inch (.5 cm) and finger press an unsewn "seam."

4. Whipstitch the two pieces together around the bottom. Work chain stitch over the seam with floss.

5. Work the remaining rows with stacked cable stitch in two colors, covering two strands of the screening with each stitch.

6. Make two 7-inch (18-cm) lengths of twisted cord (see page 6) for the decorative tie, using several strands of floss or pearl cotton.

7. For the lining, cut from fabric a rectangle 10 by 4 inches (25.5 by 10 cm), and a circle 3-1/2 inches (9 cm) in diameter.

8. Stitch the short ends of the rectangle together with a very narrow seam and overcast the raw edges.

9. Press a 1/2-inch (1.5-cm) double hem along one long edge of the piece, leaving an opening to add a drawstring.

10. Gather the remaining long edge of the piece and fit to the circle with 1/2 inch (1.3 cm) seam allowances. Stitch. Trim and overcast the seam allowances.

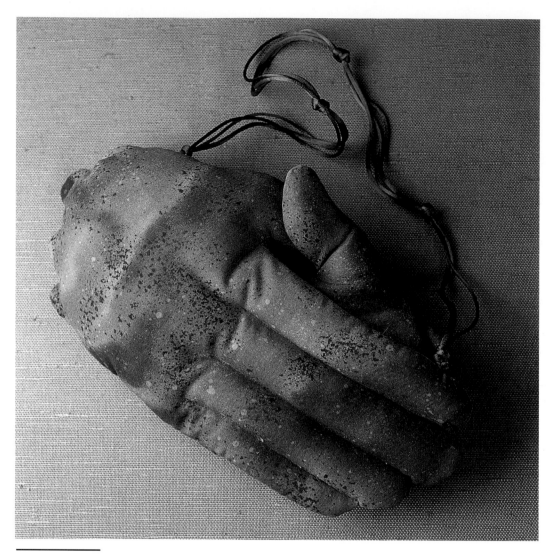

Designer: DEE DEE TRIPLETT

THE ORIGINAL HAND BAG?

Who's to say what the first one might have looked like? This interpretation makes a statement of its own, just the thing for days when you don't want to be taken too seriously. It has a practical nature, too: the size and thick padding make it just right for a large pair of sunglasses (decorated with rhinestones, of course), with room for a comb and a credit card or two.

This bag is lined with a contrasting fabric to create the inner pocket. You might add a decorative shoulder strap—we've used several strands of

rayon rattail cord—or you may omit it and use this small bag inside a larger one to protect the sunglasses or keep other small items together.

MATERIALS

Outer fabric: 3/8 yard (.35 m) for hands

Fabric for inner pocket: 1/8 yard (.15 m)

Polyester fleece: 3/8 yard (.35 m)

Fiberfill: a small amount, for stuffing

Hook and loop tape button

Ribbon or decorative cord for strap, if desired

INSTRUCTIONS

The finished bag is approximately 10-3/4 inches (27 cm) wide.

1. Enlarge and cut out paper patterns for the hands and pocket.

2. From the outer fabric, cut two pair of hands, a left and a right. Cut two pocket sections. Roughly cut four pieces of fleece as large as the hand pattern.

3. Mark the stitching line for the pocket on one right and one left hand section.

4. If a strap will be added, stitch one end securely at each end of the marked stitching line on the right side of one pocket section, strap ends aligned with the pocket raw edge.

5. With right sides together and the straight edge of the pocket toward the long side of the hand, stitch a pocket section to each marked hand section along the stitching line, keeping the strap free.

6. Trim seam allowance from the hand pattern.

7. Layer the hand sections for stitching: two pieces of fleece, hand section without the pocket right side up, hand section with a pocket right side down. Pin the trimmed hand pattern atop.

8. Set the machine for a very short stitch length. Use a walking foot or even-feed foot if desired. Stitch around the hand pattern edge, leaving an opening between the marked dots. Trim the fleece close to the stitching. Trim fabric seam allowances, and clip concave curves to the stitching line. Turn right side out.

9. To define the fingers, chalk-mark lines from fingertips to "knuckles." Fold the pocket out of the way, and stitch along the marked lines.

10. With right sides together, sew the pocket sections together around the remaining three sides. Clean finish the raw edges.

11. Stuff the hands lightly with fiberfill. Stitch the openings.

12. Hand sew the two hands together as shown in the photo, catching only the lining side of hands.

13. For the closure, sew a hook and loop dot on the outer side of each thumb.

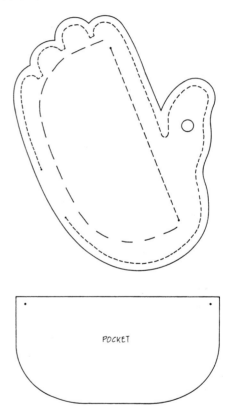

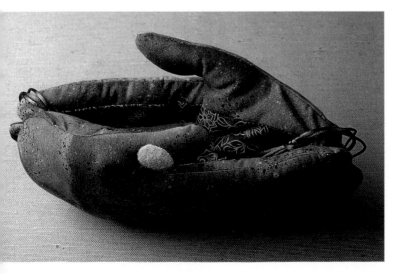

ABOVE: PATTERN, ORIGINAL HAND BAG FRONT AND BACK.
BELOW: POCKET. ENLARGE BOTH PIECES 400%.

121

A Lovely Coconut

Whether it's a keepsake from a memorable week on a tropical island or just a particularly nice specimen from the produce market, the inherent beauty of a coconut shell makes it a great candidate for creative recycling. As a handbag, it's always a conversation piece and quite practical besides.

The lining requires just a small amount of fabric, a perfect way to use up very special scraps. For the strap, we've used pearl cotton, but you might instead braid together strands of leftover yarn or pretty, narrow ribbons. Add a pair of interesting buttons, some decorative gimp, or whatever interesting materials your sewing room has to offer.

TOOLS

In addition to standard sewing equipment, you will need:

Wire brush

Sandpaper: several sheets, from coarse to very fine grit

Awl or ice pick

Saw

Drill, with 1/16, 1/8, and 1/4 inch (1.5 mm, 3 mm, and 7 mm) bits

Paste wax or neutral shoe polish

Hot glue gun or white glue

Fabric adhesive

Designer: JOYCE BALDWIN

MATERIALS

Coconut: if you are buying the nut just for this project, choose one that is symmetrical in shape and free of cracks

Lining fabric: 1/4 yard (.25 m)

Waxed linen cord or carpet thread: 1 yard (1 m), for the hinge

Pearl cotton: 3 skeins no.3, for the strap, fastener, and tassels

Decorative gimp or braid: 1 yard (1 m), 1/2 inch (1.3 cm) wide

Two shank buttons

CONSTRUCTION

Prepare the coconut.

1. With a wire brush or coarse sandpaper, remove fibers from the nut.

2. Punch a small hole in one "eye" and drain out the milk.

3. Saw the nut in half lengthwise, making the cut between the eyes at one end. Remove the meat with a sharp knife. For easy removal, microwave on high for one minute first, then allow to cool.

4. Sand the shell halves smooth with progressively finer sandpaper.

5. For a hinge at the center back, drill a row of four 1/16-inch (1.5-mm) holes in each shell half, placing them 3/16 inch (5 mm) from the cut edge and spacing them approximately 3/8 inch (1 cm) apart.

6. At the center front of each shell half, drill a 1/8-inch (3-mm) hole approximately 1/4 inch (7 mm) from the edge.

7. Use the half with the hole though the eye as the upper half, and drill a 1/4-inch (7-mm) hole at the cor-responding point on the opposite end, approximately 1/4 inch (7 mm) from the edge.

8. Wax and polish the outer surfaces of the shell halves.

Assembly

1. With the linen cord, lace the shell halves together through the holes in the backs to make a hinge. Knot the threads securely and fix the knot with a drop of hot glue.

2. Attach buttons through the holes in the fronts.

3. For the strap, twist or braid strands of pearl cotton, ribbon, or yarn to make a cord 1/4 inch (7 mm) in diameter and approximately 40 inches (101 cm) long or the desired length.

4. Thread the ends of the strap into the ends of the shell, knot securely, and fix each knot with a dab of hot glue.

The lining

1. Enlarge the pattern and cut it from paper.

2. Cut pieces of fabric from the pattern. Using 1/4 inch (.5 cm) seam allowance, sew three together, then the other three. Adjust, if necessary, to fit the halves of the nut, leaving a little excess at the edges. Press the seams open.

3. Glue the lining in place with spray adhesive. Trim away the excess fabric around the edges.

4. With hot glue, attach gimp around the inner edges of the shell, covering the fabric raw edges.

5. For the fastener, make a smaller diameter twisted cord approximately 6 inches (15 cm) long. Place the loop end over the button on the upper shell half and, if desired, add a tassel at the free end. (Tassel instructions are on page 6.) Wrap it around the buttons figure-eight fashion to close.

6. If desired, attach a tassel at the bases of the strap.

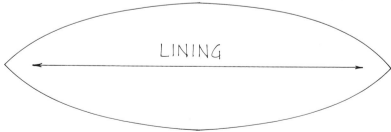

PATTERN, COCONUT LINING. ENLARGE 181%.

A PHILOSOPHICAL HANDBAG

This designer thought about purses and their purpose, and came up with a small bag that expresses a thought. Purses, at least at one time, were meant for carrying money. This one exhibits its riches on the outside for all to see (the coins are real; the bills, alas, are not). Money is also a sign of good fortune. The horseshoe shape of the bag and the horseshoe image on the back pocket continue the good luck theme. The metallic threads, iridescent fabrics, and ribbons all imply opulence, but the fabric beneath it all—a recycled painter's cloth complete with spatters—might also express a rags-to-riches theme.

The currency used here began with a photocopy transferred to fabric (custom photo shops provide this service). Some pieces were stiffened and edgestitched with metallic thread, then attached to the bag along one edge only for a three-dimensional effect. Other pieces were applied with stitching all around, with stuffing added to pad them slightly before the stitching was completed.

To make the fringe around the edge, a strip of iridescent silk was sewn into the bag/lining seam with approximately 3/8 inch (1 cm) of the silk extending. On the right side, threads were raveled from the silk to create the fringe.

While exact duplication of this bag would be quite a feat, the list of materials and instructions below will provide you with a starting point for a bag that represents the riches in your own life.

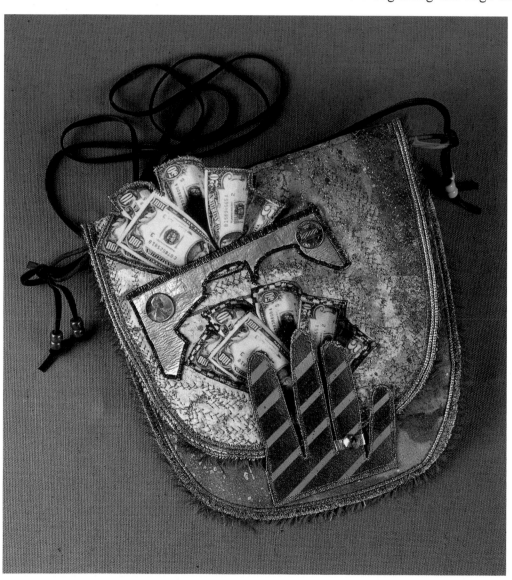

Designer: PEGGY DeBELL

MATERIALS

Fabric, for outer bag: 1/2 yard (.5 m)

Lining fabric: 1/2 yard (.5 m)

Stiff fusible interfacing: 1/2 yard (.5 m)

Assorted fabrics for appliqué

Paper-backed fusible web, for appliqué

Narrow gold braid for edge trim, 2-1/2 yards (2.3 m)

Assorted metallic or other decorative threads

Ribbons or rayon cord for strap: several pieces, 48 inches (122 cm) long

Small pony beads for cord ends

Hook and loop tape "button" for closure

Interesting beads, buttons, or other found objects for decoration

Plenty of imagination!

INSTRUCTIONS

1. For the outer bag, cut two fabric rectangles, 9 inches by 17 inches (23 cm by 43 cm). Cut two lining pieces the same size.

2. Bond stiff interfacing to the two pieces according to manufacturer's instructions.

3. Fold one of the pieces in half, then in half the other way and round the corners evenly. Use this piece to round the corners on the other rectangle. Shape the lining pieces the same way.

4. Use one of the rectangles for the bag front/back; the other will make up the flap facing and interior pocket. Cut this second rectangle in half across. Cut one lining piece the same way. Discard half of it (or use it for embellishment); the other will line the pocket.

5. Now decorate away. For appliqué, bond paper-backed fusible web to the fabric scraps, draw motifs on the paper backing, and stitch in place with metallic thread or embroidery stitches, or look at other bag designs throughout the book to get ideas. Decorate the flap facing and pocket too, keeping approximately 1-1/4 inches (3 cm) from the cut edges.

6. Assemble the bag. For the strap loops, cut two lengths of cord or ribbon 3-1/2 inches (9 cm) long. Fold each in half and pin one at the midway point of the bag front/back section, on the wrong side, loop outward and approximately 1/2 inch (1.5 cm) of the ends inward.

7. Place the bag piece and lining wrong sides together and baste close to the outer edges. If desired, use decorative stitches and various threads, and stitch the layers together in a random pattern.

8. Sew the pocket and lining with right sides together across the cut edge using 1 inch (2.5 cm) seam allowance. Trim the seam allowance, turn, and press. Topstitch the seamed edge if desired. Baste the raw edges together, stitching close to the edge.

9. Press a 1-inch (2.5-cm) hem along the cut edge of the flap facing section, or trim away that width and clean-finish the edge (decoratively, of course).

10. Place the pocket and flap facing, right sides up, on the lined side of the bag piece, matching rounded corners. Stitch them together, using any combination of decorative stitches and threads. Use an overcast stitch with a line of straight stitching 1/4 inch (.5 cm) away, or couch the metallic braid around the edge with a zigzag stitch, or use any creative finish that comes to mind.

11. Attach the strap, knotting the ends around the loops. Add beads to the strap ends if you wish, and knot below them to keep them in place.

"WHERE DID YOU GET THAT BAG?"

A beautifully decorated tin box deserves a better second life than as a repository for pencil stubs and keys to forgotten locks. It's a simple matter to add a strap and create a one-of-a-kind bag that's sure to draw admiring glances. The strap is the sort that can be rescued from a tarnished thrift shop evening bag. This box, a tiny cigar tin, has a hinged lid. If your own tin has a separate lid you can easily make a hinge. Drill small holes in the box and lid to lace the two together, as described for the coconut shell bag on page 122.

To attach a strap, solder two jump rings to the bottom of the box close to the edge opposite the hinges. If the box has been painted, sand away a small spot first at each jump ring position.

Designer: PAT SCHEIBLE

The Designers

Heartfelt thanks go to the talented designers who contributed their ideas, their skills, and their humor to the preceding pages.

Judi Alweil has a fondness for retro style and for Haitian painting, both of which have influenced her work. She designs knitted and crocheted bags and needlepoint kits through her needlecraft business, Judi & Co., in Dix Hills, NY. She is the author of *Crocheted Chenille Bags*, and is at work on a book of ribbonwear designs to knit and crochet.

Dawn Anderson designs and writes about crafts of all kinds, inspired by the view of Mt. Ranier from the window of her studio in Redmond, Washington. Her creative work has been featured in many books and magazines.

Joyce Baldwin has designed and made clothing all her life, and enjoys other forms of needle art just as thoroughly. She teaches courses in textiles and apparel at Western Carolina University in Cullowhee, North Carolina.

dj Bennett, of Lake Forest, Illinois, is a master at recreating fabrics by combining machine embroidery with a variety of other fiber techniques. Her workshops are popular throughout the U.S. and Canada. She is the author of of *Machine Embroidery with Style,* and of *The Machine Embroiderer's Handbook* (Lark Books, 1997).

Peggy DeBell, of Asheville, North Carolina, is a diversely talented artist. Her creative specialty is mixing unlikely media and found materials with brilliant and unexpected results. She focuses on clothing and jewelry, and her work has been featured in a number of craft and art books.

Sarah Douglas, particularly adept at hand needlework in many forms, views the smocking pleater as a creative tool as well as a practical one. She has taught smocking workshops internationally, and her articles on smocking have appeared in a number of publications. She is author of *The Pleater Manual*. She lives in Orinda, California.

Lois Ericson is known for creative fabric reconstruction and manipulation, for her effective garment designs, and for her uncanny ability to apply "found" objects in most unusual ways. Her popular clothing design workshops emphasize individual style and expression, an approach she also takes with her own *Design & Sew* garment pattern line. Her books include *Opening & Closing, What Goes Around, Design & Sew It Yourself* (with Linda Wakefield), and *Fabrics… Reconstructed*. She lives in Salem, Oregon.

Lori Kerr, of Durham, North Carolina, is a professional designer. She claims specialization in jewelry and textile art pieces, but experiments with just about anything that can be made of fabric. She has a penchant for machine appliqué in all its forms and enjoys sharing her skills through classes and workshops.

Peg Morris, Lake Forest, Illinois, is a gifted needleworker of many talents. She is certified as a teacher by the National Academy of Needlearts, has has taught at seminars around the country, and has appeared on the PBS *Embroidery Studio* show. She has written articles and reviews for a number of publications, and her work has been featured in needlework books such as the *Reader's Digest Complete Book of Embroidery*.

Amy Mozingo operates a dressmaking and costume design business in Asheville, North Carolina, putting to use fabrics she collects in her travels around the world. One of her special pleasures is crocheting small bags of unusual threads and yarns.

Tracy Munn has been sewing since childhood, expanding her interest into a dressmaking business in Asheville, North Carolina. In addition to stenciling and the weaving of chair seats, she has recently added reupholstery to her repertoire. She's currently at work remodeling a barn to house all her interests—and the resulting fabric collection.

Nell Paulk, of Atlanta, Georgia, experiments with just about all of the needle arts. She has applied her design talents to fabrics and yarns of every description, but is partial to out-of-the-ordinary materials and exceptional color schemes.

Anne Rubin's designs have appeared in many popular knitting magazines. She designs—and teaches—for a number of yarn companies and knitting guilds as well. For many years, she operated a successful needlepoint and yarn business.

Pat Scheible is a retired microbiologist who is enjoying, really enjoying, a second career as a decorative painter in Mebane, North

Carolina. She designs and creates with unusual fabrics, and with any other materials that strike her fancy.

Sandy Scrivano is a wizard at designing and sewing with suede and leather. Through her business, Shapes in Leather and Suede, in Carmichael, California, she creates one-of-a-kind garments for shops and galleries. Her experience at teaching the subject inspired her to develop a line of patterns especially for suede and leather. Her book, *Sewing with Leather and Suede*, will be published in 1998 by Lark Books. Special thanks to Sandy for the informative tips on sewing with leather, page 19.

Liz Spear, of Waynesville, North Carolina, produces a line of distinctive custom garments made of her own handwoven fabrics. As a weaver, she is particulary reluctant to throw away even the smallest bit of material, and sees a handbag as a beautiful way to use up the little scraps.

Karen Swing is an award-winning fiber artist, a designer of both wearables and art quilts that feature free-motion stitching on colorful fabrics. She is especially fond of making small bags—they provide a great way to use up fabric scraps and to display her collection of wonderful beads and buttons.

Dee Dee Triplett considers dollmaking her primary focus. Travels around the country to teach her craft provide the opportunity to collect still more fabric. She enjoys the challenge of creating useful articles—as long as they are visually appealing as well. She lives in Bryson City, North Carolina.

INDEX

. . .AND ONE LAST DESIGN FROM SARAH DOUGLAS, JUST FOR THE FUN OF IT: *BAG FOR THE WOMAN CHALLENGING THE GLASS CEILING*